THE
FORGOTTEN
FRONT

BRISTOL
AT WAR
1914-1918

THE FORGOTTEN FRONT

BRISTOL AT WAR 1914-1918

JAMES BELSEY

REDCLIFFE
Bristol

First published in 1986
by Redcliffe Press Ltd.,
49 Park Street., Bristol.

© James Belsey 1986

ISBN 0 948265 75 5

Typeset by Folio Photosetting, Bristol
Printed by WBC (Bristol) Ltd.

CONTENTS

ACKNOWLEDGEMENTS

My thanks to Bob Bennett for his initial inspiration. Also to
Don Anderson, secretary of the Bristol branch of the
Western Front Association, to Jerry Brookes, librarian at
Bristol United Press, and to Ava Belsey. Dean Marks has
been especially helpful with pictures and I also thank
Imperial Tobacco and Ken Pople.

Jolly outdoors army life from a 1914 advertisement.
Such innocence was soon to vanish.

INTRODUCTION

This book began, curiously enough, with the Second World War, not the First. I was researching the events of VE Day in Bristol for a 40th anniversary article for the *Bristol Evening Post* and asked Bob Bennett for help. He had drawn the artwork for the *Post's* original VE Day Special back in May, 1945.

Bob, as hospitable and helpful as always, gave me a great deal of invaluable information during a long chat. He was for many years the *Evening Post's* artist and cartoonist as well as the much-loved Uncle Bob to generations of younger readers. He had plenty to say about the day when the Second World War in Europe had ended and how the news of the great events in Europe had affected Bristolians. After we'd finished discussing VE Day and I'd put aside my notebook for a cup of coffee, he turned to me and said: 'But VE Day was nothing like Armistice Day in November 1918, you know. Now that really was a day I can never forget!'

And so the story began. He had been 18 on Armistice Day and, until Peace came, his call-up had been imminent, for Bob was a member of the Officers Training Corps based at Bristol University. His older brother Bert had already died in France — you can see his name on the roll of honour at Fairfield School in Montpelier, Bristol — and Bob could not expect to survive in one piece for very long if he followed him. Your chances of escaping unscathed in the front line were decidedly slim and the best you could hope for was a 'blighty', as they called injuries which rendered you useless for further military service but at least alive.

The Armistice lifted a terrible burden from the shoulders of this young man and, more than a half a century later, Bob could vividly recall the shattering sense of relief and the extraordinary, hysterical atmosphere in Bristol that day. The streets packed with revellers, soldiers in khaki, hundreds of wounded in their hospital blue, girls kissing every serviceman in sight, flags and bunting everywhere, tears of sorrow and tears of joy.

I have heard the identical story from others who can still remember what it was like to be in Bristol on November 11th, 1918. The celebrations went on for days and when the excitement finally died down, there was one point everyone agreed on. Nothing would ever be the same again, they said, and for once, in a period when everyone had kept getting everything so hopelessly and tragically wrong, they were right.

I was fascinated by Bob's remarks and decided to learn more about Bristol during the First World War. But then I've always been fascinated by the Great War. The Second World War seems a vast matter of technology and inhumanity; the Great War was individual men, lost innocence and a drama that has become part of our mythology as well as our history. It still has the power to haunt and touch us deeply.

I can't forget, as a very small boy, poring over heavy, leather-bound volumes of *The Sphere* illustrated magazine of 1914–1918 and staring, wide-eyed, at ghostly photographic images of shattered woods and quagmire battlefields, shell-holed landscapes and broken villages that looked like desecrated graveyards which, in a sense, they were. And time and again the faces of oddly old-looking young men gazing sadly at the camera. Later I discovered the prose of Robert Graves, Siegfried Sassoon and Edmund Blunden, the poetry of Ivor Gurney and Wilfred Owen, the paintings of the brothers John and Paul Nash, to name just a few of the artists who immortalised the war in words and pictures for future generations. How I wished I'd asked my maternal grandfather more about his days on the Western Front, because Pa did talk of stretcher bearers and duckwalks while my grandmother fumed about the 'conchies' whom she still couldn't forgive all those years later.

The Western Front has been covered magnificently. You can dip into any one of scores of minor and major masterpieces and get a strong flavour of its terrifying, troglodyte world of trenches and battle, rum and mud, darkness and wire, noise and slaughter. But what happened at home during the war, I wondered? That is a subject which has received far less attention, unlike the Home Front in the Second World War which is familiar to everyone through TV shows like *Dad's Army*, libraries of reminiscences and countless movies set in Great Britain during the years 1939–1945.

This book is not an attempt to record the full history of the home front in a British provincial city during the Great War. That's far too big a subject to tackle in such a short space. But it is an attempt to recall some of the flavour of the period, some of the long-forgotten incidents and to show how the war's legacy is with us today. I have highlighted three climacteric periods: when the war began in the summer of 1914. The first days of the Battle of the Somme. The war's ending in the late autumn of 1918. They capture the flavour of the times at their sharpest, most poignant.

My local sources are from the period: books, magazines and newspapers. I spoke to many who remembered those days but often found the war's extraordinary mythology getting in the way. It's a mythology which runs to the full gamut of legend from the Angels of Mons to tales of quite unspeakable — and, incidentally, completely untrue — German atrocities in Belgian convents. The times were so anxious, so extreme and so emotional that it is no surprise that myth, legend, superstition, propaganda and the truth have become a little blurred.

What I did discover in documents and conversations was an extraordinary epic of tragedy, irony, courage and devastating change.

James Belsey
February 1986

ONE

Countdown to Midnight: The War Begins

On June 28th, 1914, the Archduke Franz Ferdinand, heir to the Austrian throne, and his wife Sophie were assassinated by a Serbian student while on a State Visit to Bosnia, part of present-day Yugoslavia. The incident was enough to pitch an already trigger-happy, politically unstable and dangerously militant Europe into a long-anticipated war.

A furious Austria was backed by a powerful Germany, and Serbia was supported by mighty Russia. By early July, Russia began to square up to an Austria which was taking an increasingly bellicose stance towards Serbia. The Austrians claimed that Serbia had sheltered and supported the terrorist murderers of the Archduke. Germany, largely under the control of its Generals, fanned the flames. The German warrior caste bristled with ambitions to smash their way into leadership of Europe and break out of the bounds of Russia to the east and a hostile France to the west. Here was the opportunity.

In mid-July, the Balkan squabble took on a far more sinister aspect, as France sided with her ally Russia. France and Russia against Germany and Austria.

In Britain, the escalating Continental crisis was watched with serious concern, but there was more than enough to worry about at home, let alone in the distant Balkans. Britain was nearer civil war than it had been for centuries as the fight for Home Rule in Ireland led to a mutiny of Army officers at suggestions of forcing a Dublin government on the Ulster Unionists. The demands of the Catholic south for a country of their own were matched by the Unionists' shouts of No Popery. As the month ended, it took the sudden and catastrophic turn of events across the English Channel to switch everyone's attention away from the pressing Irish Question.

On July 28th, Austria finally declared war on Serbia.

Britain, despite its Irish preoccupations, moved the First Fleet to positions facing the German coast to bottle up the German navy in the event of a war.

On July 29th, Britain's Foreign Secretary, Sir Edward Grey, rejected Germany's call for British neutrality should war break out in Europe. Russia ordered partial mobilisation that day.

On July 31st, Austria and her ally Turkey mobilised. Germany refused to give Britain an assurance that she would respect the neutrality of Belgium.

On August 1st, Germany and Austria declared war on Russia. France, Belgium and Germany mobilised.

On August 3rd, France and Germany declared war on each other.

On August 4th, Germany declared war on neutral Belgium and invaded that country as part of its long-prepared plan to bring a swift, devastating military triumph in the west and so clear the way for an all-out assault on Russia. Britain responded by demanding that German troops should get out of Belgium by midnight. At midnight, with their ultimatum ignored, the British government declared war on Germany.

The German plan was to use Belgium as a back door into France and, with the French armies off-balance, to wheel a huge, strangulating loop of steel around the enemy. It very nearly worked.

TWO

Business as Usual: The First Week

Everyone in Bristol had known for years that there was going to be a war. They didn't know when or how and quite a lot of people weren't altogether sure who it would be against. It had long been part of public chatter, a bit like the weather or politics. And just as everyone knew there would be war, so there was never the slightest suspicion of a doubt that Britain would win it and that they, whoever *they* were, would be put firmly in their place. The British Empire was at its zenith and British influence was everywhere, buttressed by a thriving economy and protected by the world's mightiest navy.

When July came with its frightening, exciting, stirring news it seemed all the more of a shock because the long-prophesied drama *had* always been no more than talk or speculation. Suddenly, with a breackneck speed that took everyone by surprise, it was all coming true.

The weather in the city had been ominous for weeks. July had begun with a nightmarish thunderstorm accompanied by a whirlwind of dust, and the thunder and lightning and sheeting rain had returned again and again as the month continued, almost like a prologue to the thunder of guns that was to follow so quickly. The storms and the worsening news first from Ireland then from the Continent made everyone tense and jumpy.

As the last full week of peace began, it had become obvious that there was going to be some sort of armed conflict in Europe. On Monday July 27th the *Western Daily Press* warned its readers of 'the grim shadow of war over the Near East' and harangued the foreign politicians for 'the sheer madness of it'. The *WDP* would sing a very different tune within a week. At this stage few thought for a moment that Britain might get caught up in what had seemed a trifling row over the death of some prince or other at the far end of Europe.

But by Saturday August 1st, after five days of rapidly worsening news, things *did* start to look tricky and the more nervous souls began to be seriously alarmed. It was the beginning of the August Bank Holiday weekend, always a busy time in Bristol. The Lord Mayor, Ald. John Swaish, a Bristol outfitter, had second thoughts about taking his summer holiday but at last decided that although the news was unpleasant, he would still leave for his fortnight's break in Llandrindod Wells that Saturday morning as planned.

The city's grocers could barely cope with one of the busiest days anyone could remember, because the worsening news caused a panic among some of the better off who rushed around buying up all the supplies they could lay their hands on. The alarm spread to those who should have known — or behaved — better, because local corn merchants began outbidding each other and the price of feeding stuffs almost doubled in a day.

The Lord Mayor may have felt it was safe to leave for his holidays, but others postponed plans. People dithered and dithered and finally decided to stay. At least they would quickly hear the latest news that Bristol's newspapers were bound to print in special editions. To pass the time, many flocked to the meadows at Bower Ashton where a great International Exhibition was being held, complete with music, pageantry and displays housed in fanciful temporary buildings, one of them depicting Bristol's long-lost Norman castle.

The very first sign that the authorities in Bristol might be preparing for war came at Avonmouth docks that day. Customs officials boarded every ship in the harbour and checked for wireless telegraphy equipment. Any apparatus found was confiscated or put out of action.

There was a martial atmosphere in the city. It was that time of year when Bristol's Territorials, part-time volunteer soldiers, left shops, factories and offices for a fortnight's training in the countryside. Each man received £1 for attending camp and a fair bit of status in a country which had grown to respect soldiering and the spirit of the Terriers.

About 2,000 local Territorials were due to leave Temple

Meads station on special trains on Sunday morning. Throughout the week, their impending departure had taken on an unforeseen significance until, when Sunday morning came, it had become an important public occasion.

Sunday August 2nd began with hard, driving rain but even the filthy weather could not deter the crowds flocking to the railway station to express their feelings. People were seriously alarmed and they needed comfort.

The first group of khaki-clad Territorials to arrive on foot and by taxi cab were the men of the 4th (City of Bristol) Battalion of the Gloucestershire Regiment. They paraded smartly at 7 a.m., all a little self-conscious at the unexpected number of people who had come to see them off. There were cheers from the onlookers, manly handshakes between fathers and sons, hugs and kisses from wives, mothers and sweethearts. At 7.30 a.m. their train pulled out on its way to Minehead, where the Battalion was holding camp.

By the time the next batch of Bristol Territorials arrived, the local men of the South Midland Royal Engineers, there were even larger crowds to watch, cheer and wave. And when the people dispersed, many went off in the direction of their local church, hoping to find spiritual succour. The churches were packed, with special prayers for peace in every service, some congregations ending their hymn-singing by breaking out into spontaneous singing of the National Anthem, 'not in a triumphant but in a supplicatory spirit' one observer noted that morning.

Ernest Bevin, Bristol's best known trades unionist, wanted something more concrete than prayers for peace. He wished the city to send a hard resolution, demanding British neutrality, to Britain's political leaders. He called a meeting of workers at The Grove. Bevin, impassioned and horrified at Britain's sudden and headlong rush into war, pleaded for peace.

'We English trades unionists are on the most friendly terms with trades unionists on the Continent. It would be insane to fight with them simply because there is a dispute between Austria and Serbia' he told the meeting. He added darkly: 'The recent South African war will be a mere flea bite compared with a Great War in Europe ... should it come'.

His motion calling for Britain's neutrality was passed unanimously.

Not far away, in Corn Street, Bristol's anxious business leaders gathered at the Commercial Rooms in unprecedented numbers for a Sunday. The most influential bankers and corn merchants, insurance executives and shipping men were all there, all hoping for some news of events in Europe. Telegrams arrived every now and again and there would be calls for silence so that each cable could be read aloud. And always the same remarks repeated by businessman after businessman ... 'the stunning situation' ... 'startling rapidity of events' ... 'a bolt from the blue'. No-one could quite believe that it was really happening.

A journalist who spent the whole day in the Commercial Rooms hoping for some information about the crisis told readers of next day's *Bristol Times and Mirror*: 'The general mood among the business community is: if we are in for war, we are; we lock up the ranks and face the enemy manfully'. Or at least our sons do, he might have added.

By Bank Holiday Monday, nerves were stretched to breaking point. The weather in Bristol 'was typical of the states of the mind of the people ... uncertain and depressing ... and miserable'. The Commercial Rooms stayed open all day, while outside in Corn Street bands of young men marched up and down in high excitement. News began pouring in. The Admiralty had put an order to mobilise all Naval reserves. The Territorials had been ordered back to Bristol and their camps cancelled. The Great Western railway was cancelling all Bank Holiday excursion trains.

People wanted to show their feelings. Large throngs gathered to watch the Naval Reserves assemble in Prince Street and the RN Volunteer Reserve in Jamaica Street. When these groups set off, they were followed by hundreds and given an emotional farewell at Temple Meads. Many decided to stay to give the Territorials a rousing welcome when they made their unexpectedly sudden return from their camps, and when the men did reappear they were given a noisy, colourful reception.

Even theatre-going gave some a chance to let off steam. The Theatre Royal, by sheer coincidence, was showing a patriotic play called *Under Two Flags*, in which France and Britain were depicted as allies fighting side-by-side. At one point, the actress Henrietta Schrier, playing the part of the character Cigarette, gave a rousing speech praising the sight of an English lad and a French soldier, shoulder to shoulder against a common enemy. The audience burst into loud, spontaneous cheers and claps.

By the morning of Tuesday, August 4th it had become plain to most people that the great European war was only hours away. News of the invasion of Belgium was in all the papers and everyone had heard about the British ultimatum to Germany. No-one seriously expected Germany to back off at this late stage and anti-German feeling, never far below the surface, spread rapidly through Bristol. It would last for generations. People gathered at street corners and talked about all the things they disliked about Germans: sabre-rattling, humourless, spiked helmets, goose-stepping, arrogant and bullying. Later sadism and brutality would be added to round off the propaganda monster of the Beastly Hun, an image enthusiastically encouraged by the newspapers.

Bristol employers did their duty. It was clear that none of the city's Territorials would be back in civilian life in the foreseeable future, so firms patted the young men on the back and gave them their blessings. Imperial Tobacco was one of the first to announce that any employee required to join the Army, Navy or any national service would receive from the company whatever money was necessary to top up their service pay to the same level as their Bristol wages. Imperial also announced patriotically that it would hold open every single serviceman's job until the joyful day when he returned to Bristol.

The excitement went to many young heads. The Army had put out an appeal for volunteer tailors, clerks and others whose skills were needed at headquarters at Aldershot, Salisbury and elsewhere. Several hundred answered the call and raced off to Aldershot . . . only for some to be sent back to Bristol because of the huge number of volunteers who had got there first.

As the hours of the ultimatum ticked away, there was at

first an ominous calm. It was only when evening came that the tempo quickened as more and more people gathered on the City Centre to be near Bristol's newspaper offices. That was where the news would break. As evening turned to night, the crowds heard the presses rolling, printing the first special late extra war editions.

Rumours circulated that we were already at war. Then came a great rush as the first newsboys came racing out, weighed down with stacks of papers and brandishing placards that announced the Britain had declared war on Germany. People pushed forward to buy copies and papers were grabbed as quickly as the boys could hand them out. No-one bothered about their change. A curious silence fell as they peered over each others' shoulders, trying to read the headlines. Slowly the truth sank in and they looked up and then stared at each other in near-disbelief. Someone cheered and the cry was taken up, a deafening hurrah that echoed around the Centre. Some of the men removed their hats and began singing the National Anthem and others followed until all you could hear was the sound of men's voices. Bolder young men grabbed the newsboys' placards and waved them in the air, starting an improptu march along the pavements and roads. Others quickly fell in behind them until there was an orderly parade of shouting, cheering young men marching along the principal streets of Bristol, breaking into patriotic songs and waving their posters for onlookers to see.

No-one slept much that night. Most in the suburbs stayed up late, waiting for the special editions of the local evening papers which they knew were being printed down in the town. Some young men drank and boasted, others sat quiet and fearful. Older men discussed the politics, the righteousness of our cause. Mothers and wives shook their heads. Doors flew open when the newsboys' calls rang out at last. Again that moment of stunned silence and again that surge of emotion which reached every corner of Bristol.

Men and women reacted differently. The men were excited and relieved that the awful days of stress and tension were at last over. At least you knew where you were. Now was the time for practical matters, for the nation to take up arms.

For Bristol's women there were no such certainties. All they faced was the harsh prospect of enforced partings and frightening insecurity with the men away.

By early light you could see that Bristol was already at war. The Army's first move in the city was to take over Avonmouth docks and railway station and to start recruiting as many men as possible. Then came a call to Bristol for 1,000 horses to be scoured from local stables for work with the Army. Bristol Tramways company lost 200 of its men on the first day of the war, mobilised in the first wave of enlistment. A contingent of shoe and boot makers from Kingswood were recruited for work on Army boots and sent to Aldershot. The unfortunate officers and crew of the decidedly unwarlike German sailing ship the *Elfrieda*, which had been moored in the City Docks near the Mardyke ferry while repairs were carried out, were picked up by the police and Bristol Customs officers seized the little ship as a Prize of War. Those members of the crew who were of military age were detained as prisoners of war but the ship's officers were allowed to return to Germany when it was established that they were too old to be called up.

If anyone thought that the *status quo* in wartime Bristol was going to be the same as it had been in peace, there was a salutory meeting at the Council House, on the corner of Broad Street and Corn Street. The emergency conference was called by the Deputy Lord Mayor Cllr. C.J. Lowe to discuss the very real difficulties being created by the well-to-do with their panic buying at the city's food shops. Cllr. Lowe invited all the city's leading bakers, grocers and others in the food business to do their best to help him bring a little calm and order to what was rapidly becoming a potentially dangerous situation. Prices had risen so sharply because of the war scare that even sensible, level-headed people were now being tempted to join the scramble to stockpile as much food as possible before prices went through the roof. Bristol's Chief Constable Mr. J. Cann told the traders of his concern. He warned of the threat of riots on the streets if the panic was allowed to continue much longer. How could he police the city if the well-heeled were making it impossible for the many poor families to buy even the most basic foodstuffs? In a speech that would have been cheered at any socialist meeting he set the tone for the city's wartime mood. 'If we have to starve, let us all starve together. If we eat, let us all eat together rich and poor, and share, patriotically, the burdens of the country'.

It was enough to shame the profiteers out of their worst excesses, although high prices were to be a feature of the war. At least it gave the whiff of treason to greedy buying and price-rigging and the situation stabilised. Within days many of the country's leading food companies had taken out bold display advertisements in all the papers announcing that the products of Quaker Oats, Cadbury's, Lyons and others had not risen in price.

Within 48 hours of the war's declaration, Bristol had become one of Britain's busiest war depots. Avonmouth was an invaluable embarkation point, its six-year-old Royal Edward Dock of crucial importance to the nation's war effort. Avonmouth was well away from the dangerous, crowded Channel ports and offered the Army a good jumping-off point as well as road and rail links to London and the Midlands. By August 8th, the Army had begun to move in men and machinery on an incredible scale. One had only to look out of any office window in central Bristol to see dramatic scenes as convoy after convoy of motor lorries came grinding through the streets. They crawled up Whiteladies Road and then across Durdham Down on their way to the docks. So many lost their way in the puzzling streets of Bristol, particularly around Shirehampton and Stoke Bishop that great black-and-white fingerposts pointing 'to Avonmouth' were mounted, first in the city and then on the main roads in the surrounding countryside. Bristolians were fascinated by all this bustle, particularly when commandeered vehicles from the City of Westminster and famous London firms like Waring and Gillows came churning through. It made Bristol feel important, especially when London buses appeared, *en route* to France.

Avonmouth was soon jam-packed as the authorities funnelled more and more men and equipment into the port to meet the 30 ships which were hurrying to pick them up. Gloucester Road in Avonmouth became a gigantic lorry park while the Army hurriedly mobilised several thousand men on the dockside, equipping and organising them for the fight to come. Lord Kitchener himself, Britain's Secretary of State for War, came to Avonmouth, and pronounced himself well satisfied with Bristol's efforts.

Among the civilian population of the city, the trick now was to steady everyone's nerves and stop any silly 'mafficking', or riotous exultation. What was wanted was warlike resolve and sensible behaviour. The drapers Jones and Co. of Wine Street and High Street managed to capture just the spirit the authorities were keen to foster. Days before the expression was picked up by the Government, Jones took out big advertisements proclaiming 'Business As Usual'. Jones may even have been the first in the country to use the slogan. The cry was taken up by everyone and the wild excitement of the first hours of war began to die down.

By Friday August 7th the Lord Mayor, Ald. Swaish, was back in town, having decided that he was needed at the civic helm after all. He was hurriedly briefed on the dramas of the past few days. One matter Ald. Swaish and the other city leaders were particularly concerned about was the threat of imminent and widespread unemployment in Bristol. It was generally believed that war would cause such appalling disruption of local industries that tens of thousands would lose their jobs within a very short time. What to do about the poverty and social problems the recession would bring in its wake? Why, elect a committee, of course, and so was formed the new Bristol Distress Committee to prevent the worst excesses in case local business didn't, after all, continue as usual.

As if to emphasise the threat to industry, a meeting of one thousand men at the engineering firm of John Lysaght was held on the morning of August 7th. The management told their workers that they were being put on short time. The company normally received its supply of zinc from the Belgian city of Liège, but the German invasion had interrupted deliveries. The reaction of the men was startling. There were no grumbles, no rancour. Instead they broke into cheers, crying hurrah for King George V and his Allies.

Business as usual wasn't the only catchphrase that week.

Another was: Beware The Foreigner In Our Midst! There was a national spy-scare to match Britain's rising head of xenophobic steam, egged on by the German-bashing media. Rumours abounded that there were Hun spies at work in every city in the land and that one dastardly Boche agent had actually been arrested by detectives in Avonmouth. It was only a rumour. But three Germans were caught, three hapless sailors who were unlucky enough to be on shore leave when Bristol went to war. They were marched off to the police headquarters at Bridewell. All German citizens were ordered to report to the police immediately. Within three months every single German resident who was not a naturalised citizen had been rounded up and sent to internment camps, and those who were naturalised faced an uncertain future in a hostile country.

Patriotic gentlemen were on the look-out for any other Germans or enemy agents who might be lurking around the city. A leading member of the Bristol insurance world was stopped near the Victoria Rooms in Clifton by an odd-looking character who spoke to him in a strange accent. He asked the businessman if he had any horses to sell. 'I have none' he replied, only for the stranger to ask him for a list of all his friends who drove horse-drawn carriages in the Bristol area. 'What nationality are you?' the insurance executive demanded. 'I am German!' The police were called and the man arrested and carried off to the cells. It didn't take the officers long to realise that the supposed 'German' was a mentally handicapped Bristolian.

There was a perfect opportunity to gauge the city's mood that same day, Friday August 17th. The Government had kept the banks closed after the Bank Holiday and they were reopening for the first time. Would there be a run on money as there had been at the shops six days before? The authorities watched with trepidation, particularly since they had used the long closure as a chance to print and circulate great numbers of £1 notes. It was the first time the £1 note had been issued in Great Britain.

But by now the message had got through that panic of any sort, buying, selling or hoarding were anti-social and unpatriotic. The Bristol banks opened and the day went calmly. There was an isolated incident or two of customers asking for much more money than usual, but it only required a word or two from the clerk, a cool remark to the effect of 'Does Sir *truly* wish to withdraw such a large sum in view of the, ah, present situation' to put matters right. Embarrassed, customers decided that no, they didn't actually need so much money and took out smaller amounts.

The £1 note proved an interesting and popular novelty. Lots of customers took one or two as an unusual souvenir of the first days of the war, never expecting them to be in circulation for long. Gold sovereigns were real money, weren't they? One or two of the notes doubtless found their way to Maggs department store in Queens Road, Clifton during Saturday shopping the following day. Maggs was one of the first retailers in Bristol to realise that lots of lads in khaki meant plenty of new business lines. That day they were advertising some of the very best quality Army Sleeping Outfits to keep your son, brother or loved one dry, warm and cosy on the battlefront.

Just around the corner in Tyndalls Park Road, the British Red Cross Bristol branch held an important meeting during which they appealed to the women of Bristol to help them in all sorts of relief work. There would be clothes for our boys, food parcels for our boys and, if God so willed it, help for any of our boys who might return home injured. This last task was to become a monumental one in Bristol as the war's terrible casualty lists lengthened.

Down in central Bristol the Saturday crowds, anxious to cheer anyone in uniform, gathered to watch the exciting full-strength parade by the 4th and 6th Battalions of the Gloucestershire Regiment. The streets were lined with noisy, waving onlookers as the men marched smartly off to the Council House to meet the Lord Mayor. Ald. Swaish greeted the men and officially received their Regimental Colours, pledging to keep them in the safety of Bristol's Council House until the business of this war had been settled. Optimists thought the Gloucesters would be back at the Council House by Christmas. Realists were more troubled.

Bristol's Territorials were now in the army full-time and

unit after unit began to vanish from the city, taking young men from their pals, their workmates and their families. As the Gloucesters were handing in their colours, the Bristol Brigade of the South Midlands Field Artillery were leaving Temple Meads for Devonport. The Gloucesters left Bristol on Monday August 10th. The following day it was the turn of the Bristol squadron of the Royal Gloucestershire Hussars, the Bristol squadron of the North Somerset Yeomanry and the local men of the 3rd South Midland Field Ambulance unit. The last to leave were the Bristol companies of the South Midland Royal Engineers who left on Wednesday August 12th.

At Avonmouth the huge exercise of war proceeded as the great embarkation of men and machines and weapons continued in preparation for the landing of the first British Expeditionary Force to the continent. When the British landing came, on August 17th, Avonmouth supplied more than 2,000 vehicles, thousands of troops and great numbers of guns. At Filton, the Army were called in to mount guard on the factory of the British and Colonial Aeroplane Company. In the hospitals, at the brand new, green field Southmead centre and at the new wing of the Bristol Royal Infirmary, plans for caring for any wounded were being completed. As the first week of the war ended, the *Bristol Times and Mirror* reflected on the historic events that had come with such extraordinary speed. 'Last week was a time of unprecedented excitement in the memory of this generation, the coming and going of Regulars, Reservists, Territorials, Naval volunteers and other branches of the national services keeping the city in a state of continual bustle. There was no general tendency to panic from fear or to mafficking from joy. The citizens have kept cool'.

It wasn't true, of course. There had been plenty of over-excitement and enough mafficking to sicken that tiny minority of Bristolians who were aghast at the prospect of a murderous war, but their voices were drowned by the cheers. Bristol's leaders, political and industrial, saw that now the task was to put the city's economy on a war footing, to keep unemployment as low as possible and to find as many local men as they could for Bristol and for Britain.

THREE

Feeding the Machine: Volunteers and Conscripts

The first Bristol men, the early volunteers of Kitchener's Army, went happily, keen and eager to answer the nation's Call To The Colours. When their numbers had been wasted on the battlefield the next wave went, fearful but resigned to their fate. When they had been decimated it still wasn't enough to feed the war and sullen, unwilling men had to be dragged into uniform and shipped across to the combat zone to serve in the man-hungry trenches in a war that finally disgusted and terrified the nation.

More than 4,000 Bristol men were killed in action in the Great War. At least twice as many were wounded, a considerable number to the point of permanent mutilation. It meant the loss of something like one in 10 of all Bristol men aged between 20 and 45 and some sort of injury to one in five. It also meant that every single person in Bristol knew someone who died in the war and that most families lost a relative, a husband, a son, a brother, a cousin or a nephew. Most pitiful of all, it often meant the loss of two, sometimes three brothers at a time because brothers frequently fought side by side in the same units and in the Great War, whole units could vanish in the fiercest battles.

The first week of recruiting in Bristol was more like a farce than a tragedy. In early August, 1914 the authorities wanted all the keyed-up volunteers they could find, but they hadn't the means to cope with the hundreds who rushed to join the Army. Soon recruitment became a sophisticated and increasingly demanding machine, ultimately developing into a cold, clinical bureaucracy of conscription that plucked every available man from his home, put him in uniform and sent him, quaking, to war.

Not so in that first week, though. Until August 4th, 1914, Bristol had pottered along happily with a solitary Recruiting

Officer who sat in his office in Colston Street with precious little to do. He was helped by three or four sergeants and between them, this team was more than enough to cope with the trickle of young men who turned up to ask about life in King George V's army. The day after war was declared, the office was a complete shambles. Colston Street was besieged by scores of youths clamouring to join the army before the war ended. No-one expected it to last more than a few months. The Recruiting Officer was at his wits' end. And just as things were going from bad to worse, the army mobilised all his sergeants and he was left on his own to cope with the rush. Disappointed young men who saw the queue and realised they might have to wait for hours in Colston Street charged off to the Territorial centres, in St Michael's Hill, Park Row, Whiteladies Road and at the Drill Hall in Old Market Street.

When the first bold, exciting advertisements for Kitchener's Army appeared in the local papers on August 11th, the youthful read them with mixed feelings. 'Your King And Country Need You' . . . it was a thrilling rallying call to the excited and adventurous and an ominous challenge to the rest. Again, there were chaotic scenes, so it was decided to set up a proper, large-scale recruiting system and the Colston Hall was hired to accommodate the expected rush. The first meeting was held on August 14th and the hall was busy, but not frantically so. A lot came to watch the fun from the safety of Colston Street, causing one elderly gentleman to write to one of Bristol's newspapers: 'It is extremely irritating to see so many young men loafing around the Recruitment Centre'. The pubs near the Hall didn't complain. They did a very good trade and it wasn't considered patriotic to talk about the smell of drink, the flushed faces and the slightly tipsy behaviour of some of those who came along to enlist with their pals, buoyed up by a few beers and egged on by a strident press campaign, by over-excited friends and relations, by starry-eyed sisters keen to bask in the reflected glory of a brave brother. Bristol and Britain was decidedly for the war. It was seen as a glorious adventure, a chance for the nation to show its moral fibre. We'd become too lax, too soft, too pleasure-seeking, the patriots said. A good, clean and, naturally, victorious war would purge the younger generation of these ills.

By August 20th, 323 young men had enlisted at the Colston Hall, The Kitchener campaign intensified and the number grew to 1,000 within less than a week. The pace quickened even further and by September 2nd, a total of 2,274 men had joined up with a record-breaking day on September 1st when the recruiting staff had accepted 440. People began suggesting some sort of pals' battalion for Bristol and it seemed an excellent idea, civic leaders agreed. An approach was made to the War Office. On September 3rd, Bristol was granted permission to begin forming a 12th service Battalion of the Gloucestershire Regiment. Almost immediately it became known as 'Bristol's Own', although it attracted lads from the surrounding towns and rural areas as well as the city, like the group of 80 men who came from Weston-super-Mare to join. It was originally planned to be 1,100 strong, but that figure was increased to 1,350 to cope with the demand. Many were fresh-faced boys, not long out of school. Some were their former schoolmasters, because Kitchener's call was for an extra 100,000 men aged between 19 and 30 and idealistic young schoolmasters found his appeal a magnificent inspiration to the young, and felt they must set an example. Others were clerks, lively lads only too happy to jump at such a chance to escape the boredom and routine of their lack-lustre work. They all had a marvellous time in those early days of autumn and winter. There weren't any uniforms to start with, but there were badges to show they were recruits. It was all jolly japes and ragging, donning country clothes for route marches across Dundry Hill or parading in their smart city clothes, suits and bowler hats, for drill at the artillery headquarters in Whiteladies Road, Clifton.

At first the boys of 'Bristol's Own' were allowed to live at home and many continued to work. But not for long. The question was, where to billet the 12th Gloucester? Some suggested converting the Bristol International Exhibitions at Bower Ashton into a headquarters for the battalion. The exhibition had shut a fortnight after the war's declaration, its trade ruined by the cancellation of railway excursion trips, but the temporary buildings were still standing. The War Office thought it a splendid idea and acquired the site. The battalion moved in, using the nearby Ashton Court estate and adjoining park in Bedminster for outdoor training and the largest exhibition shed as a covered drill hall. There were pillow fights in the dormitories, bunks rigged to collapse under their occupants and a dozen more practical jokes. There were mock battles and trench digging on Brandon Hill. 'Bristol's Own' left their native city in May, 1915 with a colourful ceremony at the Colston Hall to send them on their way to their final training before combat.

After the rush to join 'Bristol's Own', recruiting fever died down and by the middle of September, alarmed at the high cost of hiring the Colston Hall, the War Office decided to move recruitment to more modest premises in the Guildhall where the decreasing number of volunteers were easily coped with. From then on it did not matter how hard local patriots tried to egg on young men to join up. Youths who had stayed behind and ignored Kitchener's Call were determined to avoid going into khaki. The former Tory Prime Minister Arthur Balfour, vice-president of the Central Committee for National Patriotic Organisations, came down to Bristol in mid-December to address a great recruiting rally at the Colston Hall. He hectored the audience: 'There is not a man of us who would not lay down his life gladly ... Germany will never be everything while there is one cartridge left and one stout heart left'. A considerable proportion of his listeners clearly disagreed with that first sentiment. About one third of the 5,000 or so who had crowded into the hall were men of military age. Only a tiny handful stepped forward to enlist.

The year ended with rather more down-to-earth suggestions on the problem of Bristol recruitment from the city's patriotic fortnightly magazine *Bristol And The War*. The Christmas issue editorial said: 'Sufficient is not made of the jolly adventure of soldiering. One would think, to hear some people, that it consisted of nothing but impaling Germans on bayonets and spending the intervals in starving and shivering in flooded trenches. Give our modern buccaneers some glimpse of the glories of travel, change of scene, and camp-life, which is assuredly part of the business of war. And — this is important — dilate a little upon the smartness of uniforms, the excellence of rations. Let the men have a glimpse of the wonderful machinery of the war . . . the rate of fire of a machine gun. Let us come down to talk which will be understood by the young men who do not remember much history, who never read anything but football returns in Monday's papers. Men who do not profess to follow or understand modern politics, yet who are quite prepared for any amount of strenuous knocking around in search of a fight — it matters little to them who they fight or why!'

It didn't work. And through the next year the Government slowly began to realise that if not enough men were prepared to volunteer, they would have to bring in some form of conscription. It was a controversial move, because people of all parties objected to the very idea of conscription. The idealists felt it sullied the nation with its undignified coercion of unwilling men. The trades unions saw it as a threat, fearing that military conscription would usher in some form of industrial conscription with workers put on army pay and their lives governed by army discipline. But despite the objections, a national register of all men over the age of 16 was eventually drawn up in August 1915, along with a military register of all men aged between 18 and 40. Now at last the authorities could identify every last bit of cannon fodder in the land.

Next came the Derby Scheme; a neat piece of moral blackmail. Lord Derby's plan was simple. Don't actually *force* anyone to enlist, just get each man of military age to 'attest', that is to pledge to serve his country if and when he is needed. To soothe any troublesome critics, the Derby Scheme included a special appeals procedure so that if a chap had a good reason not to go to war — say a large family to support, a family business which would collapse if he went away or important war work — he could appeal against his call-up and receive a proper hearing. If he made a good case, he would be exempted. Thousands of men went along to 'attest' at the Colston Hall in the dying weeks of 1915. The most frantic day of all was Sunday, December 12th when more than 5,600 pledged to serve if and when needed. In quite a number of cases, after talking things over with the helpers who were running the Derby Scheme in Bristol and having a word or two with one of the Recruiting Officers who were always on hand at attesting sessions, men decided to enlist. They saw that military service was imminent and preferred to volunteer rather than be forced into the war. Not enough, however, to satisfy the generals' demands for more and yet more soldiers.

The second stage of the Derby Scheme, once men had attested, was a rolling programme of call-ups. First the youngest single men would be made to honour their pledges and then the system would progress through successive age groups to the oldest. And once all the available single men had been called up, the Scheme would then turn its attention to the married men. With an appeal tribunal, of course. Ald. John Swaish, who had just completed two years as the Lord Mayor, agreed to become chairman of the Bristol Local Tribunal which would hear any appeals against call-up. He and his fellow Tribunal judges must have been among the most unpopular men in Bristol. The tribunals dealt with 22,000 cases in Bristol before the war ended and only 5,600 men were granted exemption and allowed to stay at home.

The Derby Scheme hadn't really worked, but that was all part of the Government's confidence trick. The authorities could prove it too, because they had those invaluable registers, compiled the previous August. Nationally, only about half the single men and less than half the married men of military age had attested. Since it clearly wouldn't be fair to call up any married men until all the available single men had joined the services, surely some sort of compunction should be introduced? By the beginning of 1916 the politicians had skilfully made conscription the only possible solution to the problem they had deliberately created with the Derby Scheme.

It was just a short step to the Military Service Bill of January, 1916. The Bill decreed that all single men aged between 18 and 41 were deemed to be in the Army Reserve and would be called up in their successive age groups. This at once set the single men against the married men.

Why should husbands receive preferential treatment? That was quite possibly the Government's intention, and the generals must have been even more pleased when local tribunals up and down the country granted exemptions to so many single men, for one reason or another, that they could loudly proclaim that not nearly enough men had been found for the Army. So, to settle any arguments, in June 1916 an act was passed which deemed that all men, married or single and aged between 18 and 41, were in the Army Reserve. Now the generals had a pool of millions of men to call upon, with only Ald. Swaish and his tribunals, which were retained from the Derby scheme, to save you from the Army.

Conscription set family against family and friend against friend in Bristol, just as it did everywhere in Britain. Why on earth should those strong, healthy young men who worked in the City Docks or at Avonmouth be allowed to stay at home while the fathers of large families were sent to join the Army? Why should the city's coal miners escape call-up while those with family businesses were ordered to France? Why were Bristol's tough, fit young shipbuilders and repairers given permission to remain in Bristol, earning good money, while professional men were forced out of successful careers to sit shivering in flooded trenches?

Even worse was the Bargains Department, an astonishingly divisive scheme only seen in Bristol. Bristol companies made written returns of all their employees who were of military age and these were then submitted to the tribunals. Companies were given permission to 'bargain' the employees they valued and trusted most against those they were happy to see the back of, or needed less.

It was such a touchy matter to be a young, fit, obviously healthy man in Bristol that if you worked in any of the essential war industries, you began to need some form of protection against silly young women who thought it patriotic to hand out white feathers accusing you of cowardice or those who had lost relatives or had sons in France and who made angry remarks in the street. So came the issue of official badges, 'badges against badgering', although even these were scanty protection against the mute bitterness of the bereaved who began to hate the sight of young men in civilian clothes. For a while Bristol police joined in the pestering too, stopping any clearly healthy young men who were not in uniform and demanding to see cards which exempted them from military service. This pernicious practice was quickly stopped because although it unmasked one or two 'shirkers', it mainly publicly humiliated and shamed men who had perfectly good reasons not to be in uniform.

Only the most essential workers were allowed exemption as the war progressed. Before it was over, some 60,000 Bristol men had been in the services and most of them had witnessed some of the horrors of this ghastly war. The experience was to scar the minds of a sizeable minority of two generations of Bristolians.

And what about those pioneers, those brave lads who had been the first to go to war, the ones who had fooled about at Bower Ashton, marched and sung lustily on jaunts across Dundry, drilled at Whiteladies Road and become the very emblem of Bristol's pride in her sons? 'Bristol's Own', the 12th Gloucesters, arrived in France with a complement of 27 officers and 886 men on November 21st, 1915. They broke them in gently with a spell on the then quiet Somme sector in early December, later moving them to Arras in the spring and early summer of 1916. The Battle of the Somme began on July 1st and the battalion was moved back there on July 20th. By the end of the month they were at the front, facing the notorious Delville Wood or Devil's Wood, as it had already become known. 'Bristol's Own' received their first full blooding in trench warfare on September 3rd, 1916 when they took part in a murderous attack on the strongly-held German positions near the village of Guillemont. In the brief action one officer and 44 men were killed and another 48 were missing. Six officers and 225 other ranks were wounded. From a total of 913 men, some of the brightest, keenest, bravest young men in Bristol, 324 had been killed or injured in their very first real taste of full-scale Western Front action. Such was the Battle of the Somme.

FOUR

July 1st 1916: The Hundredth Week

The long-prepared German plan to smash France in August 1914 had failed. The German advance had hit stubborn resistance from both the French and the unexpected British Expeditionary Force, just when it seemed that victory was in sight. Germany's huge attacking army had to crash hastily into reverse and the British and French allies took advantage of the enemy's set-back to launch a series of damaging counter-attacks as they tried to outflank the Germans. Then the Germans tried to outflank them. Outflank attempt followed outflank attempt until both sides glowered at each other across a battlefront that stretched from Switzerland to the English Channel. They dug in.

Within weeks they had dug in so deeply that stalemate was reached. By the beginning of 1916, the war on the western front had become an *impasse* with two vast systems of trenches and defensive strongholds facing each other across a deadly no man's land. The question was — how to break out?

Germany's generals decided that the solution was an assault on the ancient fortress town of Verdun in north-eastern France. They argued that France would rush in all the troops she possibly could to defend the town and save her national pride. Germany would turn Verdun into a 'mincing machine' to devour the French army and thus leave the way clear for an advance. They attacked in February, 1916 and the casualties were colossal. A million men of both nations died at Verdun in 1916. France turned to her British ally for some relief from these hideous losses and Britain responded with plans for an offensive on the River Somme.

Throughout the last week of June, 1916, British artillery launched a ceaseless barrage along the Somme front. It was designed to destroy the great barbed wire entanglements

Arthur, the proud volunteer, in his smart new 'Bristol's Own'
uniform with the Avon Gorge in the background. Beyond his
Christian name and the date, December 1914, no further details are
known. Nor his fate.

YOUR KING AND COUNTRY NEED YOU

THE

NEW BRISTOL BATTALION
GLOUCESTERSHIRE REGIMENT

To the Mercantile and Professional Men of the City of Bristol and Neighbourhood.

Lord Kitchener has sanctioned the enrolment of Single and Married Men of the City of Bristol and Neighbourhood between the ages of 19 and 35, who are willing to join the Colours for the duration of the War. The Battalion is to be a Battalion of Mercantile and Professional young men, under Officers of the Regular Army.

CONDITIONS :—

Married men are eligible and get separation allowance.

You must be between the ages of 19 and 35.

You agree to serve for the period the war lasts.

You agree to serve at Home or Abroad as may be required.

Clothing and Equipment will be supplied free by the Government.

Full Army pay.

The Battalion is to be an Infantry one, and will constitute a unit of the Regular Army.

Seven days' notice of calling up will be given.

If you wish to serve your Country in this time of stress, obtain the necessary application form at the New Battalion Offices, Colston Hall, Bristol, or any of the Bristol Banks, fill same in and send to

THE CHAIRMAN,
Bristol Citizens' Recruiting Committee,
New Battalion,
Colston Hall, BRISTOL.

AN APPEAL TO EX-N.C.O'S.

LORD KITCHENER appeals to Ex-Non-Commissioned Officers of any branch of His Majesty's forces to assist him now by re-enlisting at once for the duration of the war.

PARTICULARS.

Chiefly required to act as drill instructors. Promotion to non-commissioned rank immediately after enlistment. Age no obstacle so so long as competent. No liability for service abroad if over 45. Pensioners may draw their pensions in addition to pay of rank at Army rates.

Apply for information to
MAJOR CARR,
8, Colston Street.

GOD SAVE THE KING.

Above: The call goes out. September 1914.

Opposite Top: Weston-super-Mare's 80 volunteers answering the call for 'Bristol's Own' Battalion, arriving at Temple Meads station on November 9 1914 to take up their billets at headquarters at Bower Ashton.

Opposite Centre: Recruits at Bower Ashton in October 1914, returning from rifle drill. The fanciful buildings of the International Exhibition were already commandeered for Army training and billets.

Opposite Bottom: Early days. October 1914 and the raw recruits of 'Bristol's Own' receive first rifle instruction. Uniforms would come later and there would be little opportunity to pose for the camera.

Overleaf: Front and back pages from the heavily censored patriotic magazine *Bristol and the War.* It tried to keep up an optimistic mood but as the war progressed the obituaries increasingly dominated the pages.

Published Fortnightly.   **PRICE ONE PENNY.**

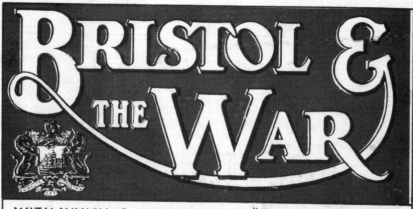

BRISTOL & THE WAR

WITH WHICH IS INCORPORATED "THE BRISTOLIAN".

Vol. 1. No. 4.   NOVEMBER 14, 1914.

THE "BLACK WATCH" IN BRISTOL.

[Photo, E. C. Stevens. Arley Hill.

MARCHING TO COLSTON HALL.

THE above contingent of that famous Scottish Regiment, the "Black Watch," arrived at Bristol from Salisbury Plain on the morning of Tuesday, November 10th, and marched through the streets to the skirl of the bagpipes to their billeting quarters at Colston Hall. Considerable interest was evinced by the people on the line of route in the appearance of these sturdy soldiers of Kitchener's army, who bore unmistakable evidence of having roughed it during their month or two's sojourn on Salisbury Plain, and much satisfaction was expressed in their ranks when the order came for their departure to more comfortable quarters at Bristol. These men form the new Battalion of the "Black Watch," many of them being still attired in civilian garb, but as to the general excellence of their physique there can be no question. They carried all sorts of kit, and as they passed along at a swinging stride the crowds that had gathered gave them a rousing reception, at which the men appeared greatly pleased.

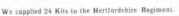
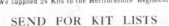

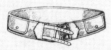
Printed by **RANKIN BROS. LTD., Trenchard Street, Bristol,** for the proprietors, The Colston Publishing Co., Ltd. 4 Colston St., Bristol

Above: The Colston Hall with desks and staff ready to receive men 'attesting' their willingness to be called up under the Derby Scheme. Conscription for all single men came first with conscription for married men following six months later.

Below: Former Prime Minister Arthur Balfour addressing a huge recruiting meeting at the Colston Hall in December 1914. The meeting was a dismal failure, with only a handful of the 5,000-strong audience volunteering. Notice the Indian Mutiny and Crimean War veterans under their banner (upper left).

Above: 'Bristol's Own', the 12th Glosters, parade on Deanery Road outside the Royal Hotel in early 1915 not long before being sent to France. More than a third of the battalion were killed or injured in the first full blooding in the Battle of the Somme on September 3 the following year.

Below: Funeral parade of the 12th Glosters in Victoria Street on February 23 1915 following the death of 40-year-old Private Bowen of pneumonia. He was buried with military honours at 'Soldiers Corner' in Arno's Vale Cemetery.

Ald. John Swaish, Bristol's Lord Mayor for the first two years of the war and then chairman of the Tribunal which considered men's appeals against conscription into the Army.

that protected the enemy trenches from any infantry assaults, and to kill as many Germans as possible. But despite more than a million shells, the wire wasn't completely cut and, although they had suffered horribly from the deafening, terrifying days and nights of the artillery onslaught, the German battalions were largely intact. They had been protected by deep chambers dug into the chalk. When the bombardment suddenly stopped at 7.30 a.m. on Saturday, July 1st, it was clear that the British were about to launch an infantry attack. The Germans raced up from their dug-outs to man machine guns, rifles and artillery. They were well in time to meet the lines of British soldiers walking slowly towards them. The hail of machine gun fire that followed was almost impenetrable. The generals could hardly believe the losses when the figures were at last compiled. On July 1st, 65,000 British soldiers were killed or wounded.

By the end of the Battle of the Somme in November, 1916, more than a million men, British, German and French, had been killed or wounded.

Bristol couldn't hear the distant rumbles of the huge British artillery barrage as they could in some South Coast towns late at night that last week in June, but echoes of the action quickly reached the Bristol newspapers. It was becoming clear that the long-awaited 'Big Push' by Kitchener's Army of volunteers in France and Belgium was about to begin and the city, which had so often been packed with troops in the last year or so, was suddenly almost deserted of men in khaki.

On Saturday, July 1st, at the very moment that the British troops began clambering out of their trenches to start that fatal walk towards the German lines, families in Bristol could read cheerful news from France in the local morning papers. It was reported that 'high explosives have ranged over the German trenches for the past five to six days' and that 'hopes are again raised high'. But this was matched with a warning. 'The public should not pitch their expectations too high or look for any immediate or decisive results'. Wise advice, as things turned out.

Bristol in the summer of 1916 would have seemed shockingly different to anyone who had known the pre-war city. All building work had come to a halt. The roads were often choked with vehicles plastered with big red crosses and travelling in convoys through the city centre. An enormous red cross waved over the new wing of the Bristol Royal Infirmary. Then there were all those strange men shuffling around the city in the blue uniforms given to the war wounded. You could see them, often on crutches, making their way into the Bristol Hippodrome or the local cinema, or visiting the zoo in Clifton. Above all, there were women at work in the most public and surprising places. They were delivering the post, serving behind shop counters, even driving vans around the city, all of them unheard-of occupations for women or girls just a couple of years before.

One woman's name was on everyone's lips — the name of the unlovely D.O.R.A., unlovely, of course, unless you were a sanctimonious do-gooder or busybody, prude or killjoy. D.O.R.A. wasn't actually a person but an armoury of home front legislation called the Defence Of The Realm Act, which had been introduced on August 8th, 1914. She had absolute power, from censoring the newspapers to switching off street lights.

By 1916 D.O.R.A. had rubbed away many of the brighter, noisier, rougher traces of peacetime Bristol. Some of her first victims were the pubs, and it wasn't perhaps such a bad thing. Bristol's pre-war pubs had been pretty loathsome places and the city's drinking habits excessive during the daily licensing hours from 6 a.m. to 11 p.m. By July, 1916 the pubs could open only from 12 to 2.30 p.m. and from 6 to 9 p.m. The buying of rounds was strictly forbidden. Too many civilians had tried to salve their consciences by 'treating' men in uniform, and the Army was tired of seeing men staggering back to headquarters after an evening out on the town. If you wanted to take home a bottle of Scotch or gin, you could buy it only between the hours of 12 and 2.30 p.m., and then only on weekdays. These drastic cutbacks in the licensing hours had been ordered in an effort to improve industrial efficiency, and they worked. Drunkenness, such a familiar and depressing sight in old Bristol, became something of a rarity and it wasn't just because the men were away either. The incidence of female drunkenness fell sharply too.

Crime figures tumbled correspondingly, making Bristol's streets safer at night for longer than anyone could remember. Safer from crime, that is, but far from secure for pedestrians trying to pick their way home along uneven pavements in near pitch darkness. Bristol had a nightly black-out now and the ruddy glow which had once lit up the sky had vanished for fear of night-time attacks by zeppelins, aircraft or even naval bombardment, as had happened on the east coast of England and in London. Houses and shops were forbidden to display lights after dark and street lamps were either left unlit or painted blue so that they gave no more than the faintest glimmer of light. Since it was believed that zeppelin crews could guide their huge aerial machines by loud noises from the land below, all Bristol's chiming clocks were silenced after dark and none of the churches could ring their bells.

This catalogue of gloom ran on endlessly. There were coal shortages and food shortages. Travel restrictions and inflation. High prices and more and more demands for men for the services. The raised prices and shortages had affected Bristol's old age pensioners and those on fixed incomes most of all. The old people's State allowance of 5s (25p) a week had become pitifully inadequate by the summer of 1916 and in June Bristol's Board of Guardians, who acted as a last safety net against starvation, began what later became a successful campaign for the old folks' pensions to be raised to 7s 6d (37p) a week.

The weather had been dreadful too. June seemed to have been nothing but rain and cloudy skies and the old people and the more credulous muttered and complained about the guns in France. It was all those bangs and shells and bullets that were ruining the weather, creating all this extra moisture, they said. But despite the weather, the restrictions, the call-up of men, the irritations and the hardships, most people were still firmly behind the war. Even the Labour Party, which, with the trades unions, had been among the most vociferous opponents of the conflict. Labour held its annual conference in Bristol's Victoria Rooms in January, 1916 and the crunch issue was whether or not the party would support the coalition government's conscription efforts and war aims. The vote went the Government's way.

The same patriotic, warlike mood showed only too clearly when Bristol City Council held its June meeting. The city had been presented with an exciting war prize by the 4th Gloucesters, the 'Bristol Bantams', in the form of a captured German machine gun. This was placed in full view in front of the Lord Mayor as the meeting began.

All of which meant precious little sympathy for any shirker or slacker. 'Scrimshanker' was often the word used. And little sympathy for any 'conchies', the derisive term for conscientious objectors who refused to take part in any warlike activities. There was, however, one exception. The week the Somme barrage began, Bristol was agonising over the case of one particular local 'conchie' locked up in Horfield Barracks. The young lad was called Lees and he came from the little village of Hallen, near Avonmouth. He wouldn't join the Army because he believed all killing was wrong, so he was thrown into jail. At Horfield Barracks, Lees had been kept in solitary confinement in a cell six foot by 11 foot. There was a tiny table and three planks for a bed with a small window high up on one wall. He was fed on bread and 'skilly', a watery soup made from meagre vegetable and meat remains. No one was allowed to see him for the first eight days of his confinement, and he was forbidden letter-writing material and any books. His Bible was removed. It was this last act that brought the matter to the notice of Parliament. The boy's mother, when at last given permission to see her son, was horrified to find him 'being driven mad by isolation' and the authorities were shamed into restoring his Bible and improving his rations. They deliberately chose, however, not to allow him a knife, fork or spoon. He must eat with his hands, a calculated insult in such a manner-conscious age.

If the public hated 'conchies', they despised shirkers and people took vindictive delight when one was winkled out to be exposed to public ridicule and shame. The police had picked up several that week and they were hauled before Bristol Magistrates on Saturday July 1st to answer charges that they had changed addresses without informing the authorities, thereby hoping to escape call-up. One was 32-year-old Arthur Crick, who had moved to North Street, St James without notifying the powers-that-be. He admitted the offence but pleaded in mitigation that he had a mother and six young children to support. It cut no ice with the bench and he was fined 10s (50p) and placed on the register for conscription. By then there were too many heroes to think about, too many glorious young men, too many brave deeds to allow the least pity for the slackers and the 'conchies'. A whole new keyed-up, epic language had been created and polished to describe the war, its combatants and its victims.

Men didn't die. They made 'the supreme sacrifice'. They were the 'fallen'. Everyone in an Allied uniform was a 'warrior'. Volunteers were 'plucky' and 'staunch'. You didn't join the Army, you were 'Called to the Colours'. You weren't brave, you were 'gallant'. Any quick military movement was 'swift' and even the slightest hint of a British victory, however small, was a 'conquest'. Even the enemy, despite being derided as the 'Hun' with all the feral implications that description implies, was the 'foe'.

More and more men from Bristol were making that supreme sacrifice by the summer of 1916. In home after home there was the tragedy of loss or the anxiety over a wounded son or husband. If loss, it was always accompanied by a comforting letter from a commanding officer. These letters speak volumes about the war, or how the front line troops felt the war should be portrayed to the civilians at home in Bristol.

These are extracts from just a handful of such letters sent back to Bristol during 1916:

'His conduct under my command was always most gallant, he was much admired by all the section and most popular with all ranks' . . . 'Unassuming always, he was one of my bravest and hardest workers' . . . 'Always open hearted, kind and considerate' . . . 'One of the cheeriest and most amiable chaps in the platoon' . . . 'On all occasions, under the greatest stress possible, he always had shown himself calm and collected and courageous' . . . 'It may be some consolation to you to know that your son's splendid heroism will live with us always as a magnificent example of self-sacrifice and devotion to duty' . . . 'the whole section fought to the last man and everyone, except one, was either killed or wounded. Your loss and mine is the nation's gain. He was a lovable boy and a keen and willing soldier'.

And few had suffered any pain, the letters said. He had been hit on the head by a bullet. He had been hit by a shell. He had been hit directly through the heart. Why tell the truth, the officers said. The men readily agreed to keep silent. No matter that the lad had been left dying of agonising wounds in no man's land.

If there was pain before death, then that was heroic too. Take the Bristol man, aged 21, who had been a clerk at W.D. and H.O. Wills and who had been trapped on barbed wire during a German bombing raid on the British trenches in March, 1916.

'He alone held a trench with a rifle and hand grenades against an onrush of Germans for such time that his comrades retreated to a safer position, not stopping until he was seriously wounded. He was then overpowered and taken prisoner and when the enemy were driven out of the trench, they left him as dead. The Corporal at the Dressing Station told me that he was very cheerful and apologised for being such a trouble to him. So passes away a man who was a comrade in distress; a cheerful and willing soldier'.

The war knew no barriers in its increasing list of victims. Young officers led their men from the front in daring attacks and fought shoulder to shoulder with them in defence in the trenches. Shells and bullets made no discrimination between ranks. In the summer of 1916, as the Somme offensive approached, there were scores of Bristol families in mourning. The Sheriff of Bristol, H.E. Chattock and his wife were grieving over the death of their second son Reginald, a 2nd Lieutenant in the 4th Gloucesters. He had been killed in France. He was just 19 years old. Bristol Rugby Club members were dismayed to hear that the popular Gladstone Brindal of Fairfield Road, Montpelier, had died of wounds. He had regularly turned out for the club's 2nd XV and had been a likeable companion to his fellow clerks at the Midland railway. Plumber Harry Bubb from St Agnes had died of wounds after being hit by shrapnel on guard duty. Lorry driver H. Harrison of Dundridge Road, St George had been killed when his truck was hit by a shell. Rifleman Arthur Galop of Filton Avenue, Horfield had died of wounds near Ypres. Harold Rich of Belmont Road, Brislington had been killed by a German catapult bomb in France. And so the list went on, a Roll of Honour that appeared day by day in the local papers. The big battles to come would make those lists of the spring and summer of 1916 seem miniscule.

Those who had suffered wounds at the front which were considered severe enough to warrant being sent back to Britain for hospital treatment could well find themselves in Bristol. The city had become one of the main war hospital centres by the summer of 1916. This fact added an extra urgency to the annual meeting of the Bristol branch of the Red Cross at their headquarters in Clifton on Thursday June 30th. Saturday July 1st would mark the start of the 100th week of the Great War and it was a good time to review their work so far. Members heard that since the outbreak of war, Bristol's Red Cross volunteers had been on duty at Temple Meads station to help with the transfer of 20,364 wounded soldiers from their ambulance trains to the war hospitals in and around Bristol. If you included other transfers they had been involved in, the Bristol Red Cross had helped transport and meet more than 33,000 men. It was a matter of great pride, the meeting was told. They couldn't guess that the city's Red Cross volunteers were about to face a week that would leave them physically and emotionally shattered, their strength and their feelings stretched to the limit by night after night of trying to do something to comfort the broken survivors of the disastrous British offensive.

Domestic matters, little problems about help at home and help on the tramways, whether football was really all right as a spectacle in war-time, these were the small preoccupations of Bristol as the 100th week of war began on Saturday July 1st, 1916.

Bristol Tramways and Carriage Company was desperately short of drivers and was advertising for any men who would be prepared to work either on the buses or on their fleet of taxi cars, with driving tuition thrown in for free. But, the advertisements stressed, the only applicants who would be considered were those able to prove they were either over military age or had been officially declared ineligible for the Army.

Domestic servants were in short supply too, for there were too many well-paid jobs vacated by the young men to make domestic service in the least bit attractive, despite live-in wages of £22 or so a year.

Bristol City Football Club held its annual meeting that Saturday and the club's chairman, just like today, was complaining about the problems caused by 'the debt hanging around our head'. But at least one much more contentious problem had been removed from the world of football at last. In the early months of the war, the killjoys had attacked the soccer clubs for continuing to play at a time when so many sporting activities had been stopped. It was disgraceful, they said, to see such public entertainment. The times were far too serious for such frivolity and, in any case, who was playing the game and why weren't they in uniform fighting for King and Country rather than Bristol City? It was little use City and Rovers repeatedly arguing that they were only fielding scratch sides, not holding men back from the war, and that anyway they were more often than not playing against service teams and giving bored soldiers stationed in the Bristol area something to shout about away from the tedium of army life. Now at last the football world could defend itself. City's chairman Mr. D. Murdock told the meeting: 'The war problems have exercised my and my brother directors' minds as to the advisability of carrying on the game. But any doubts have been removed now that every eligible man between the ages of 18 and 41 is in the Army. The playing of football gives pleasure to thousands, aye, tens of thousands of their flesh and blood in the trenches as they read of the doings of the club they support'. Football would carry on as best it could, and with a clear conscience.

That night the local stalwarts of the Red Cross were back at work at Temple Meads station, greeting the ambulance train which pulled in at 8.30 p.m. The transfer of the 90 injured men from the train and then by car and motor ambulance through Bristol's rainy streets to the Beaufort War Hospital in Fishponds went as smoothly as ever.

At 10.50 p.m. any remaining shop and house lights were switched off.

The first wounded men who had survived the initial attack on the German trenches early on the Saturday morning reached Bristol within less than 48 hours, their uniforms still dusty and chalky from France. The casualties arrived in an ambulance train which steamed into Temple Meads station at 4.30 a.m. on Monday July 3rd from Southampton docks. Ninety-six of the men were still able to walk and tottered across the platform to a welcome cup of tea and a small snack, perhaps a piece of cake. Then they were led to waiting lines of cars and ambulances.

A further 100 soldiers were too badly hurt to move themselves and were carried on stretchers. Those who could speak coherently told the Red Cross workers that they couldn't describe the deafening, terrible effect of the week-long British artillery barrage. No words could begin to give an impression of living alongside such a nerve-wracking noise.

A single hospital could not cope with the sudden influx of

200 more wounded, so they were dispersed, to the Bristol Royal Infirmary, Southmead Hospital and the Bristol General Hospital. Word had come through that there were more casualties heading Bristol's way.

A few hours later, Bristol readers sat down to thrilling news in that morning's newspapers. It was all glorious stuff. The official *communiqué* from the British army headquarters in France, issued the previous Saturday, announced that 'many prisoners have already fallen into our hands and, as far as can be ascertained, our casualties have not been heavy'.

The postal service from Bristol and the rest of Britain to the Western Front, even during battles, was remarkably swift and efficient. It would only be a few days before the local press would reach young Bristolians in the battle zone, sent by proud relatives who drew attention to how the good old *Western Daily Press*, *Bristol Evening News*, *Times and Mirror* or *Times and Echo* was so faithfully reporting these momentous events. The reports at first brought gasps of disbelief from the soldiers who had actually witnessed the army's monumental balls-up, as the lads were describing it to each other ... and then cynical laughter. It wasn't the fault of the censored media, but even in the 1980s, British journalists still suffer the after-effects of that moment of disbelief and the cynicism that followed. You cannot believe what you read in the papers, can you?

News got around Bristol that another ambulance train had arrived, but at least there was a chance to forget the war for an hour or so because the summer sales began at opening time on Monday, with shops like Taylors on College Green advertising items at 'pre-war' prices. The sales were a great success, shoppers coming from all over town to find bargains at a time of very high prices.

Taylors' management were a little uneasy about all these young women staff behind their counters. Although some of the prices may have been at pre-war levels, the service wasn't what it used to be, they felt. Their valued customers deserved something better ... the sort of service that their male assistants had offered in happier times. They issued a public apology: 'Due to the absence of male staff we must admit some little deficiency in serving the great crowds of customers but the firm appreciate the patience and indulgence shown by the public.' The girl shop assistants' reaction to the statement was not, of course, recorded.

Monday meant back to business for Ald. John Swaish and his local tribunals, making judgements on a rash of cases of younger men who had appealed against call-up. One lad told Ald. Swaish and his panel that all three of his brothers were now serving in the army, leaving him alone to care for their elderly parents. He was also regularly sending parcels of food to his brothers to ensure that they were fed properly. Ald. Swaish turned to the military representative, Captain Reeves, to ask for his opinion in this second matter. Capt. Reeves was astonished. 'This is the first time, sir, that I have ever heard it said that soldiers serving in France have needed food sent to them by their friends.' The lad's appeal was refused and he was conscripted.

Throughout the day, there was great excitement about the latest snippets of news of the big battle taking place in France. More and more heard that another hospital train was coming to Bristol and several hundred lingered on to greet the invalids.

The ambulance train arrived at 7.20 p.m., this time carrying 350 injured. They were all 'sitting up' cases, none of them too badly hurt to require more than a helping hand to the refreshments being handed out by volunteers before they were taken to the 40 vehicles waiting to take them to the Beaufort Hospital. As they appeared, they were loudly cheered and many of the men waved back, however exhausted and shaken they all were.

Clifton Caterers did their calculations at the end of a very busy day. During that day alone they had supplied the volunteers at Temple Meads station with 200 lb of cake, 210 buns and cones, 34 lb of bread, 10 lb of butter, 10 lb of coffee and tea, 36 lb of sugar and 10 gallons of milk.

So far only the less seriously wounded men from the Somme attack had reached Bristol, those the medical orderlies in France had been able to ship swiftly out of the battle zone and who had been well enough to travel at once. But the badly broken men, those who needed more treatment before they could face the journey back to England, were not too far behind.

It was clear that the British army must have suffered losses in such a large-scale operation and no-one was very surprised when the Roll of Honour, published on Monday, revealed that 143 officers and 1,612 men had been killed or injured. By Tuesday, the figure had fallen to 102 officers and 682 men killed or injured. The figures were tragic, of course, but such were the facts of war and the British public bore the figures stoically. Those who were not being hopelessly optimistic began to realise that despite the published figures, which announced the sort of losses to be expected in the long-awaited 'Big Push' by Kitchener's Army, something was wrong. Perhaps one of the first signs came in the Bristol papers on Tuesday July 4th, with an official announcement that 'the arrival of wounded in Bristol will be an almost daily occurrence now'.

The next ambulance train arrived at Temple Meads station at 11.25 p.m. that Tuesday. The Red Cross and their fellow volunteers were there and now the seriousness of the battle in France was becoming clear. The train carried 105 wounded and only 11 of them were able to sit up. The rest lay on stretchers or on officers' cots. The men were counted off the train. There were 31 officers. It was the largest number of injured officers Bristol had received on any train. Most of the troops were North Country men. They still smelt of battle and their uniforms were stained. Some were in severe pain and the teams who helped them to the waiting ambulances did their best to comfort them.

One Red Cross worker asked one young lad how the Battle of the Somme was progressing, explaining that the newspapers were only giving the sketchiest information. The battle seemed to be going well. 'The war's going to be over in a few months', the young man said. Why did he think that? 'Oh, because of a remark made by a German prisoner who said they could not last out much longer'. This struck the right note and was given wide publicity.

The chirpy mood, underscored with a sense of purpose, determination and righteousness, was kept up by the newspapers of Wednesday July 5th. Everything was proceeding according to plan and the Somme was the scene of great events, with our troops consolidating their gains of the past days. One eye-witness report of the great British advance of the first day of the battle was published. It revealed: 'The men dropped in all directions from machine gun wounds but happily, fatal wounds were not numerous'. Nothing to be too alarmed about, in fact. That day's Roll of Honour announced that 105 officers and 1,527 men had been killed or injured.

Dr. Barclay Baron, the Lord Mayor, and the Lady Mayoress decided it was time to put in a formal appearance at the old Platform, 6, Brunel's original station, where the ambulance trains were received. They went down to meet the train due to arrive in the early evening. It steamed in at 8 p.m. Bristol's Chief Citizen and his wife watched as almost 200 troops were helped off the train. It was an arduous business. More than half were too badly hurt to walk and had to be carried away. The others were able to take advantage of the usual refreshment stand with food and hot drinks laid out ready for them. All the men were suffering from machine gun or rifle bullet wounds or shrapnel injuries or all three. Bristol's subdued Lord Mayor who knew all about illness and pain through his work as a physician, had to steel himself to put on a brave face confronted by such a heart-breaking sight.

On Thursday July 6th Bristolians tried to forget the ghastly procession of ambulance trains and the convoys of ambulances ferrying the latest wounded men to the area's war hospitals by throwing a big celebration for more than 1,000 men who were well on their way to recovery from injuries suffered in action before July 1st. Great crowds of soldiers in the distinctive hospital blue were taken to Clifton Zoo which, like cinemas and theatres in the city, offered free entrance to the injured. Despite the rain and the sinister whispers that all wasn't as well as it might in France, it was a jolly occasion with scores of helpers determinedly serving refreshments and ensuring that our heroes had a good day out.

That day the Bristol press admitted that the German Army had been prepared for the British attack and had not been caught by surprise. That was by now obvious to anyone living in the Bristol area. The sheer numbers of war wounded arriving daily from France were tragic evidence that neither the Germans nor their machine guns had been wiped out by the great artillery barrage.

By the weekend the Red Cross and St John Ambulance workers, the women of the Voluntary Aid Detachments who served refreshments and the rest of the team at Temple Meads were exhausted but the tempo quickened again, with three trains arriving on Saturday and Sunday, July 8th and 9th. They brought another 576 badly injured troops for Bristol's rapidly-filling war hospitals to cope with.

By Monday July 10th, 1916, the Roll of Honour was starting to creep up. That day's figure of killed and injured was 419 officers and 2,066 men. The scale of the losses was starting to dawn on the public in Britain and the nation's war hospitals found themselves with more patients than ever before. And these weren't tough, cynical, horny-handed professional soldiers, or most of them weren't. They were that first wave of volunteers who'd answered Kitchener's call, the flower of the nation's youth, as they would soon be known. At least these had survived. Their less fortunate comrades lay dead in France.

One of the first families to hear the worst were the Moores of Chandos Road, Redland. They received a letter on Friday July 7th regretting to inform that their son, 2nd Lt. Ernest Moore, had died of bomb wounds less than a week before. He was 27 years old. Identical letters were on their way to tens of thousands of homes in every city, town and village in Britain.

FIVE

Women Step In: The City at Work

First the authorities fretted over the virtue of Bristol's women in a wartime city and tried to keep them at home. Then they lured them into work for the war. Finally, they dismissed them from the factories and sent them packing back to home.

By the end of 1914, Bristol had become a garrison, its streets often packed with strangers in uniform. More than 10,000 soldiers arrived that winter to take up quarters away from cold, wet, windy open-air camps in such inhospitable areas as Salisbury Plain. You could hear regional accents from every corner of Britain and some from the Commonwealth, too. Hardly a week passed without a new body of men arriving, fit and healthy after long weeks of training in the fresh air. The Scots were the largest group. Several thousand Kitchener's Army volunteers from North of the Border came to Bristol. The world-famous Black Watch took up quarters in the Colston Hall. Other public buildings like the Victoria Rooms and the former roller skating rink, the Coliseum in Park Row, became billets too.

All of which quickly had self-appointed watchdogs of the city's moral well-being tut-tutting and clucking about the dangers of so many young men let loose in a strange city. The matter was raised by the Licensing Justices. Perhaps it would be better if they removed temptation from the lads' way? It was agreed. All pubs were ordered to close by 9 p.m. It was planned as a temporary measure but before long early closing had become a national institution. That dealt with the temptations of the bottle and prevented any unwanted late night carousing in Bristol's alehouses and gin palaces. But what about the young women?

'It is alarming to see the way in which young girls are losing their heads and forcing their attentions upon soldiers in the city's streets and parks,' one shocked Committee member of the Bristol Vigilance Society told the group's January 1915 meeting. Unless action was taken, there was bound to be a decline into immorality and a boom in unwanted 'war babies' they said. In fact, in the first two years the illegitimacy rate fell. The authorities sent women police patrols into the main streets and most frequented parks, moving on any groups of girls they found flirting with soldiers.

The Vigilance Society was wrong in its prediction of an immediate 'war baby' boom, but right in its other warning. The moral climate was changing rapidly, not so much because there were so many soldiers around but because of women's attitudes. The war put them to work and showed them new worlds of freedom and independence. Ironically, the only fears concerning work at the start of the war were of severe unemployment. Police were privately horrified at the prospect of trying to keep law and order in what many experts prophesied would rapidly become a destitute city, its industries and commerce ruined by disruptions in Europe. Unemployment spiralled during the early weeks and it looked as if the very worst fears were to be confirmed. But then the figures levelled off and began to fall as Bristol switched its efforts over to a war economy that brought great industrial success.

The city was ideal as a production and distribution centre. The new Avonmouth dock was a modern, efficient port well away from the dangerous North Sea and the crowded Channel ports. There was a thriving boot and shoe industry. Expertise in aviation. Engineering skills and an expert knowledge of chemicals. A tobacco industry. Clothing factories. Above all, excellent communications by road, rail and sea.

Before long it wasn't unemployment that posed the problem. It was lack of hands to tackle the huge contracts that poured into Bristol. Avonmouth's Royal Edward Dock was six years old when the war began and within hours it had more trade than it knew what to do with. Great convoys of vehicles trundled through the city and across the Downs, London buses, furniture vans, guns drawn by caterpillar tractors, lorries and cars. In Shirehampton there was the

Above: Bristol Postwomen outside the central Post Office in Small Street in the spring of 1916. Milk and letter deliveries were among the first previously all-male jobs taken on by Bristol's women as more and more men were called up.

Below: A formidable column of 500 Land Army women marching to the Colston Hall in February 1918 behind a boy's band.

Above: Nurses and patients at Bishop's Knoll in Stoke Bishop, a mansion run as a 100-bed private hospital by the Bristol philanthropist Mr R.E. Bush with his wife acting as quartermaster. It was one of the best-known and best-liked hospitals for Australian troops throughout the war.

Below: Early 1916 and an ambulance train has just pulled in at Temple Meads station. The stretchers with pillows and blankets ready are to ferry men unable to walk to the ambulances waiting outside on the station incline.

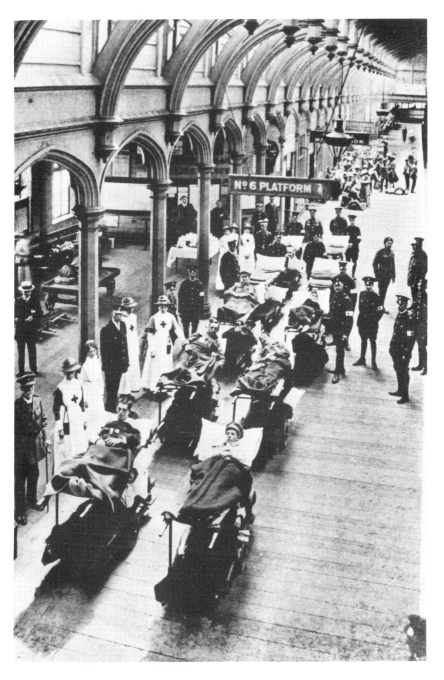

Platform 6 at Brunel's original Temple Meads station shortly after the arrival of yet another ambulance train. Cot cases lie on double-decker stretchers while the walking wounded (background) await transport to hospitals in Bristol.

Above: A sad picture which epitomises the strength and fortitude of those who had suffered. Summer races at the Beaufort Hospital in 1916.

Below: A stoical group of Australian 'walking wounded' in the Beaufort assembly hall.

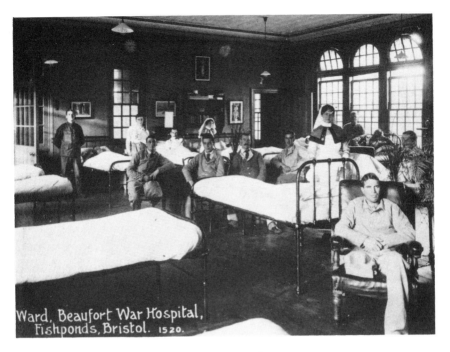

Above: The Male Convalescent Ward.
Below: The Beaufort had to utilise all available space. The doors on the right led to padded cells, used in the asylum days.

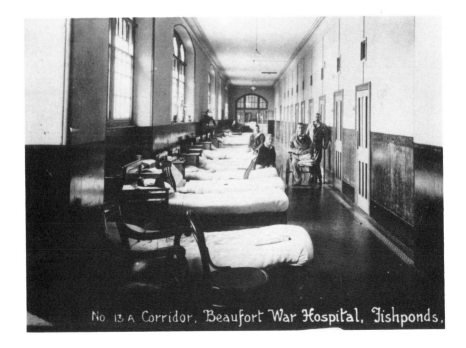

Above: King George V visiting the Bedminster factory of W.D. and H.O. Wills in November 1917 during a tour of local factories.

Below: King George V meets war victim George Maggs at the Wills factory. Maggs lost both his legs early in the war. George Wills (centre) watches.

'Sacred to the memory of Bristol's sons and daughters who made the supreme sacrifice". Field Marshal Sir William Birdwood unveils the Bristol war memorial on June 26 1932.

Right: H.S. Dancey, chairman of 'Bristol's Own' Old Comrades Association, places a wreath on the Glosters Cross in 1930.

Below: 'Bristol's Own' veterans return to the Somme in 1930 with the Glosters Cross in the background. The cross vanished during the Second World War and a replacement is being mounted to mark the 70th anniversary of the Somme battle.

ceaseless whinnying of thousands of horses being checked
and cleaned at the Remount Depot which sent 347,000
horses and mules to war overseas via Avonmouth before the
war ended. Train after train packed with troops arrived at
Avonmouth station from every corner of the country and
later hospital ships berthed, unloading their pitiful cargo of
men injured in distant theatres of war.

The war made the aviation industry rich. The Filton
works of the British and Colonial Aeroplane Company
manufactured 50 of the successful two-seater Bristol fighters
a week, running a second factory at the Tramways workshops
in Brislington in an attempt to keep pace with demand. By
the end of the war, they were also building a 'bloody
paralyser', a plane with the strength and range to achieve the
ultimate — to bomb the Hun in Berlin. In early 1915, once
the soldiers had left, the Coliseum became an aircraft
factory for Parnalls. Every now and again they'd stop traffic
in Park Row to allow a smartly turned-out seaplane to
depart from the works.

Within days of the war's declaration, the local shoe
industry had won gigantic orders for army boots from the
French government and before the war ended Bristol had
supplied millions of boots for British, French, Italian,
Serbian and even Russian troops.

One social habit which changed during the Great War
was the increase in cigarette smoking, and the tobacco
industry thrived. The British–American Tobacco Company's
Ashton Gate factory poured all its efforts into cigarettes and
tobacco for the military while Wills made mountains of
packets of Woodbines and Gold Flake for the lads in the
trenches. One Army padre became nationally known as
Woodbine Willie because he reckoned the temporal pleasure
of a drag on a Woodbine was of more immediate help than
the spiritual aid of a prayer for any wounded man in his care
on the Western Front.

Ploughshares needed to be speedily turned into swords,
particularly to satisfy the demands for shells and high
explosives. Every factory which could help with the furious
munitions effort was pressed into service, full-time or part-
time. Bristol Gas Company began using by-products to

make explosives for bombs, grenades and shells. It's said it made the street lights even dimmer than they already were. More than 60 companies in the area turned out shell cases on any spare machinery, Wills among them. The big soapworks on Broad Plain stopped making soap and concentrated on the manufacture of 'dynamite glycerine'. After the Germans launched their first gas attacks, Britain needed a reply. A mustard gas factory was set up in Avonmouth, just another part of an enormous industrial effort.

This quickening tempo of work and a very real desire to get on with the job to help the country and to support pals and mates at the battle front brought a startling slackening of friction between managements and unions. You could see the signs right from the start. A couple of minor strikes in Bristol ended the week the war began, workers deciding it was their patriotic duty to swallow differences with the bosses. Trades unions were among the last important groups to oppose the war. One trades unionist retorted to the propaganda poster of the little girl asking *What Did You Do In The War Daddy?*, 'I tried to stop the bloody thing, my dear'. But by the time the TUC held its annual Congress in Bristol in September 1915, it was policy to support the Coalition Government while attacking 'the sinister efforts of a reactionary Press' in the campaign to introduce conscription. Lloyd George, then Minister of Munitions made an unscheduled and typically extrovert appearance and was allowed to address Congress. He called for fewer restrictive practices and his speech was given a polite hearing. Later, when Parliament investigated the munitions industry, it was shown that the unions had already voluntarily relaxed many rules to speed production of armaments. Labour and management needed each other like never before and union leaders who had previously been seen as militant rabble rousers became respected members of the war-time team.

Just how far middle-class attitudes had changed was shown dramatically at a private meeting called by Dr. Cyril Norwood, headmaster of Bristol Grammar School, in 1916. On the evidence of what was happening in the factories, he believed all workers should be compelled to join their respective unions and that 'black-legging' and any form of under-cutting should be outlawed. The headmaster of one of the West Country's most famous schools was urging the closed shop!

This honeymoon was a feature of the war. The Adult School Union and the Workers Educational Association ran a rest house, Penscot, in the little Mendip village of Shipham. Here workers' leaders and some of the more idealistic industrialists met for informal talks, 'struck by the growing feeling that every possible attempt should be made to give permanence to the better understanding that has grown up during the war among many employers and trade union officials'. The better understanding would ensure that, when the time came, women would be forced to realise that they had no place in the all-male scheme for post-war industry.

In the first heady, patriotic days of August 1914, hundreds of women stepped forward to offer any help they could. There was plenty to do too. There was welfare work with the Red Cross and, most immediately, a desperate need for volunteers to greet and care for the flood of Belgian refugees arriving in Bristol. There were the families who had managed to get out before the German advance. Bristol played host to more than 2,000. The Belgians were quickly found homes, in big houses like those loaned by the owners in Victoria Square, Clifton, in hastily-converted centres like the Imperial Tobacco Company's sports pavilion and in private homes with families who offered a room or two.

For younger, really adventurous girls there was the challenge of nursing. Within weeks of the outbreak of war, a group of nurses from the Bristol Royal Infirmary had volunteered and left for France.

As more and more men were called up, women took their place. At first in the less physically demanding jobs like serving behind shop counters or working as clerks in city offices. As the *Western Daily Press* wrote in 1916: 'For some months, local employers have been responding well to appeals to get women to work and young lady clerks are no longer a novelty. Female shop assistants are now engaged in numerous shops formerly staffed by men. It is no longer uncommon to see a young woman driving a tradesman's motor van and driving it very well'. That was just the start. Middle-class girls who in peacetime would have been locked away in the drawing rooms of the smarter suburbs, their only escape into marriage, found freedom. They could become postwomen, clerks, tram conductresses and even factory workers. Working class girls who would have been employed in poorly paid drudgery now found well-paid jobs in industry.

There was even money for the children. Boys and girls aged 12 to 14 were allowed to work 33 hours a week. Thousands earned at least £1 a week in the local munitions industries. Those over 14 did even better, creating a population of teenagers with money to spend. They were the forerunners of the affluent British teenager.

Mass training schemes were set up. One centre was at Horfield, where Bristol Corporation had a half-completed baths complex which had only reached the roof-and-walls stage when all building was stopped by the war. It was clean and dry and the Munitions ministry converted it into a temporary Instructional Factory., Here relays of women and children were taught simple engineering operations, one move at a time! Rather than train them in complete engineering skills, a long and expensive business, they were taught a couple of basic assembly line tasks. It meant that they could start being useful the moment they arrived at a factory. But lots of companies were too eager for hands to wait for even minimally trained workers. They took on anyone who would work and trained them themselves. The women showed they could do a hard day's physical labour.

Women also showed considerable courage in dangerous places. The most hazardous was the Mustard Gas factory at Avonmouth where shells were filled with the toxic gas. Accidents were frequent, giving workers a terrifying taste of what the front line troops had suffered. Almost 1,300 were badly gassed at the factory, 140 in one incident alone.

King George V and Queen Mary came to the Bristol area in November 1917 to tour important factories. 'In accompanying the King and Queen in Bristol' an observer noted, 'a visitor could not help being impressed by seeing great workshops, equipped with all sorts of mechanism, manned — if this word may be used — by young women'.

Long before the women's Land Army was formed in April, 1917, women had gone to farms in the suburbs and surrounding countryside to help as hay balers and field-workers, gardeners and tractor drivers. Once the Land Army began, even more joined, helping at market gardens as well as farms. Although male agricultural workers were often protected from call-up, the need for more and more food became pressing as imports were cut to a minimum by the enemy submarine blockade. In February 1918, 500 local Land Workers marched through the city to attend a conference at the Colston Hall to lend their support to calls for even more food production. They used the parade as a recruiting drive, urging women to sign up at their local employment exchange. The rally was well-timed. It coincided with a scare on the labour market. The Bolshevik revolution in Russia the previous October had led to cancellation of all Russian contracts. Women were thrown out of work without notice. This new breed of woman wasn't, however, to take such treatment lying down. They vented their anger on Employment Exchange officials who were 'subjected to considerable unpleasantness and even vilification'. Within weeks they'd found new jobs, on the land, in new munitions factories, at the Royal Aircraft Depot at Yate and other centres. But the experience left a bitter taste. There could be few illusions about what would happen to their well-paid jobs when the men came back.

This was reinforced in those informal chats in the Mendips between management and unions. They actually put their thoughts in writing in early 1918.

'The position of woman as an industrial worker is and always must be of secondary importance to her position in the home. To provide the conditions which render a strong and healthy family life possible to all is the first interest of the State, since the family is the foundation stone of the social system. While women have helped and are helping the nation splendidly, they must realise that men have not forfeited their jobs by answering their country's call, and doing work which women cannot undertake'.

Meanwhile the work and money gave women a self-confidence never known before, and they showed it. Clothes changed and became more practical. Hairstyles were no longer so painstakingly fussy. Cigarette smoking, almost unheard-of among women before the war, became common enough by 1918 for Wills to prepare certain brands aimed specifically at the female market. The moral ground shifted too. Before the war working class boys and girls in the crowded inner city knew plenty about sexual matters but middle and upper class girls grew up in a strictly Victorian atmosphere. If boy did meet girl, there was always a chaperone around to watch for any improprieties. The war changed all that.

There were opportunities to be out and about and there was the charged atmosphere of the war itself with its freedoms, its endless partings, its apparently infinite appetite for the corpses of brothers, boyfriends and acquaintances. Everyone knew someone who had been killed. How could *your* body be the Holy of Holies if men's bodies were so cheap? There wasn't a convincing answer. There was a passionate mood of here-today-gone-tomorrow and, for the first time, there was a chance of affairs without pregnancy. Male contraceptives, available only with the greatest difficulty before the war, were now sold over many shop counters and love affairs which would have stopped with sighs and kisses in peacetime became physical.

From the middle of the war, as the sexual revolution gathered pace, illegitimacy figures began to rise and, by one of those strange twists that is so much part of the Great War's story, the country minded far less than expected. A feeling had grown up that Britain needed babies and folk were being far less fussy about whether those babies were conceived in wedlock or not. Married women found new lovers with husbands away for months on end. Affairs sprang up in their thousands, between women factory hands and the few remaining men workers, between housewives and soldiers stationed in the city, between caring helpers and the war wounded they were looking after. When infidelities were discovered, it often led to violence.

A notorious case was that of Private Albert Cross of the Gloucestershire Regiment. Cross, a 32-year-old former painter and decorator, shot his 27-years-old wife Bessie with his army rifle on the platform at Temple Meads station while waiting to catch a train to London *en route* to France on October 15th, 1917. She died of wounds at Bristol General Hospital. She was several months pregnant by a married man. Cross had been home on 10 days' leave from the front. The two appeared to have had a peaceful time at their home in Henry Row, Baptist Mills and he seemed to have resigned himself to her lapse. She had accompanied him to Temple Meads to wave him goodbye. Cross missed an earlier train and was waiting for the 3 a.m. when the shooting happened. Bristol Magistrates Court was packed when he was remanded to appear at the Bristol Assizes. Everyone noticed his strikingly bronzed appearance, still deeply sun-tanned from his months in the open air in France.

The war's effects on morals were apparent the moment the Assizes began. Lord Justice Coleride spent the first day clearing up two cases of bigamy before turning to the pathetic matter of a 27-year-old servant who admitted trying to conceal the birth of her male child. The baby's body was discovered in an outhouse and medical evidence showed the child had been born healthy. The woman wept so loudly and bitterly at the end of the trial that it took several minutes before the judge could make himself heard. She was sent to prison for a month.

The Cross case took up day two, November 22nd. Scores of people were turned away from the jam-packed public gallery. Cross had lost much of his sun-tan after more than a month in the cells, but his story had lost none of its local impact. His defending barrister asked a court clerk to read aloud letters his client had written to Bessie from the trenches. He himself could not bear to read them for fear of breaking down with emotion, he told his lordship.

'Bessie, my love, you have brought sorrow to us all ... could not you have seen this when this dirty cur of a fellow was after you ... if you knew what we have to go through, you would have gone straight but the damage is done now ... ask God to pray for you and I will pray for you as well, Bessie ... try to be a different woman for the children's sake and mine'.

All ammunition had to be handed in before leaving France, so why had that bullet been in the breech? It must have been an oversight, an innocent mistake, defence counsel claimed. A witness described seeing Cross and his wife talking on the platform. She saw him raise the rifle as if 'acting in fun' when there was the crack of a shot and the woman slumped. The jury took 90 minutes to find Cross not guilty of wilful murder and the court erupted into cheers and hurrahs. It took minutes for angry officials to restore order.

For men pursuing women who would not go to bed with them until their wedding night, bigamy was an easy option with so many people on the move. It took the courts years to clear up the mess of bigamous marriages between local girls and soldiers who had passed through the city.

A new woman emerged in the war years and a lot of people did not like her. They begrudged such women their independence and they disliked their brash, outspoken manners. They disapproved of their clothes and appearance, the shorter skirts, the shorter hair and the way Land Workers wore trousers off as well as on duty. When peace came, many of the freedoms vanished as quickly as they had come. Women's hour was over for the time being and there was little in the way of consolation as a male-dominated establishment stampeded them out of jobs and back into the home or domestic service. But they could no longer deny women the vote. On February 6th, 1918, women over the age of 30 were granted suffrage. And it could never be argued again that women were not capable of doing men's work.

SIX

War Casualties: Bristol's Ghostly Freight

The war was not even a month old when the first front line victims began to arrive in Bristol. At first they were a sad but stirring novelty, pained, pale faces glimpsed through the windows of the rare ambulance trains or momentarily seen in passing vehicles en route from Temple Meads station to one of the local hospitals. Well-organised little bands of volunteers and medics were formed to meet them, small convoys of Red Cross and private vehicles were organised to transport them and hospital beds were put aside to nurse them back to health after their ordeal.

Within weeks it had become horribly clear that Bristol's — and, for that matter Britain's — preparations were pathetically inadequate. No-one, not the generals, nor the politicians, nor the soldiers and certainly not the British public had any conception of how appallingly heavy the cost of the war was going to be in numbers of dead and injured. This was the world's first, bloody, full-scale experience of mechanised, industrialised warfare and from the very first day to the final shots just before 11 a.m. on November 11th, 1918 there were few generals who managed to shake off dogmatic faith in the mass infantry attack as the only possible answer to a well-defended enemy position. Such assaults may have succeeded in the days of cavalry and musketry and limited artillery. In the age of the machine gun, the full-frontal infantry attack was at worst a murderous impossibility and at best a sickeningly costly way of advancing just a few yards into enemy-held territory. A machine gun's rapid fire, ranged fan-like in a repeatedly traversing arc that merged with similar arcs from fellow machine guns to left and right, created an almost impenetrable barrier of flying steel. To that you could add the terrible bombardments of shells of every shape and form from an increasingly sophisticated artillery and the constant threat of snipers' rifle shots of pin-point accuracy. And as if all that hail of metal wasn't enough, there was the hideous threat of blinding, choking gas.

It meant casualties on a hitherto unprecedented scale. The Bristol area, which started the war allocating 520 beds for any military who might need attention, ended up with 15 times as many and even then, when the slaughter reached its ghastly crescendos during the Battles of the Somme and Third Ypres, or Passchendaele as it soon became known, there were barely enough beds, nurses or doctors for all the patients.

On August 6th, 1914, just two days after Britain had declared war on Germany, the Bristol branch of the Red Cross offered the brand new wing of the Bristol Royal Infirmary, opened in memory of the late King Edward VII, as a Base Hospital for the military. The offer was immediately accepted and the wing, with its 260 beds, was swiftly re-equipped for its new purpose with emphasis on the sort of treatments which would be necessary for dealing with bullet and shrapnel wounds.

Out in the pleasant agricultural countryside to the north of the city, the Bristol Board of Guardians, the body which looked after the very poor, were adding finishing touches to a little hospital which they had built to cater for up to 260 sick paupers. The Guardians patriotically offered the use of this new Southmead infirmary, as it was called, to the military. That was accepted too.

The excitement of those first heady days of August was barely dying down and the mood of 'business as usual' just starting to take its place when Bristol first came face to face with the realities of the wounds of war. The very first men to be sent to the city's two hospitals were survivors of the British Expeditionary Force's first encounters with the enemy. These were all tough, professional soldiers and they were greeted with sympathy, admiration and not a little satisfaction when it was seen how efficiently Bristol was coping with her little groups of heroes.

One typically cheery anecdote did the rounds ... about the regular soldier who had kissed his wife goodbye in Bristol and set off with the BEF to fight the Hun. She had barely had time to settle down to her existence without him when there came a knock on the door and a messenger announcing that her husband was a patient at the Bristol Royal Infirmary. He had re-joined his unit, been shipped across the Channel, wounded and brought back home in a matter of days. She took a good deal of convincing before she would accept that it wasn't a practical joke, the story went. *That's* the sort of prompt attention our few brave lads unfortunate enough to get hurt can expect, everyone agreed heartily.

The story sums up the optimistic spirit which prevailed as everyone rolled up their sleeves to do their bit, to greet and care for the few, inevitable casualties of what was surely going to be a brief and victorious campaign against German militarism.

The trickle of injured began to turn into a stream. Bristol's very first ambulance train came steaming in from Southampton on September 2nd, before the war was even a month old. It carried 120 survivors from the gallant action at Mons when the British Expeditionary Force had helped halt the German advance on Paris. Further trains were expected. It began to dawn on the authorities that the provision of 520 beds for the sick and wounded might not be so generous after all. So they made Southmead bigger and soon that wasn't enough to meet the demand. Public-spirited individuals offered the use of their homes, notably the philanthropist Mr R.E. Bush who paid for the conversion and running of his mansion Bishop's Knoll in Stoke Bishop as a 100-bed hospital throughout the war, his wife acting as quartermaster. Bishop's Knoll was to become one of the best-known infirmaries for Australian troops. Hospitals opened in public buildings and large mansions, in stately homes like Ashton Court, which became an officers' hospital and even schools, like Red Maids. Biggest of all was the Beaufort War Hospital in Fishponds, now Glenside hospital. It had been the Bristol Asylum before the war. Its inmates were dispersed to other asylums and the buildings converted for wartime use. It went into action with 1,460 regular beds and, at a pinch, it could take 1,640 wounded at any one time thanks to 180 emergency beds laid on the floor. And they were used too.

Well over 100,000 patients were cared for in the Bristol area before the war ended and if the hospital regime was strict and straightforward, it was magnificently efficient.

Those first men arrived by day but as the situation worsened, the trains came in later and later until most arrived in the early hours of the morning, unseen and unheard by the sleeping city. The wounded were like some ghostly freight, to be ferried in while the main lines and the main roads of the city were at their quietest. It was only at the height of the worst battles that urgency demanded that trains came in as quickly as possible, regardless of day or night.

The trick with all the tens of thousands who arrived each year was to make these shocked, disoriented lads feel secure and at home as quickly as possible. Few of the wounded who arrived were locals and quite a number came from homes thousands of miles away in Canada, Australia, New Zealand and, after 1917, from the United States.

The place to begin the end of that trauma was at the point of arrival in the city, and Bristol developed a superbly disciplined, brisk and successful welcome. Even at the worst times, during the Somme and Passchendaele, the system worked perfectly. However dog-tired the nurses and doctors, ambulance drivers and stretcher porters, tea ladies and Red Cross volunteers — and during critical periods it was common to go without sleep for 48 hours — there was always the discipline of the system to fall back on.

Military precision and orderliness were the rule at Platform 6 where the ambulance trains pulled in.

First. Position ambulances and cars at the ready on the incline outside the station. Inside, lay tables with refreshments and prepare rows of seats. Place stretchers at regular intervals along the platform and check that each has a clean, white pillow.

Second. As the train is signalled, Red Cross nurses and ambulance men to fall in at their officers' orders. VAD ladies to fall in behind their refreshment stands, tea and coffee on the brew. Others with the regular gifts to incoming wounded to take up pre-arranged positions along the platform. The train pulls in slowly. At the windows of the train many soldiers are to be seen. To the unaccustomed visitor it is a time of great stress of feeling and of tightening of the muscles of the throat. Some of the soldiers smile, but many look tired and weary.

Third. Help the walking injured off the train, lead them to chairs and, once all are seated, hand out a packet of cigarettes, boxes of matches and a clean handkerchief to each man. Then a cup of tea or coffee and something to eat for each man.

Fourth. While the walking injured sip tea or coffee, remove severely wounded from train with the utmost care and gentleness and place them on waiting stretchers. Each to be given cigarettes, matches and a handkerchief and any man unable to light his own cigarette through incapacitated limbs or loss of limbs to be offered lighted cigarette.

Fifth. All walking injured to be given postcards to write to inform relatives that they have arrived safely in Bristol. Postcards to be collected, and then walking injured led to waiting cars.

Sixth. Repeat drink, snack and postcards for cot cases and then remove them to ambulances and so to hospital.

Seventh. Above all, be friendly and smiling, prepared to listen and talk. Many men will wish to talk and will be happy to answer questions now that they are safely in the care of friends at home.

It was true. Many of the wounded were bubbling over with chatter, so delighted and relieved that the nightmare of attack and a wound, stretcher bearers and a hasty dressing, trains and boats and trains was at last over. They showed war trophies, a German officer's hat, a German soldier's cloth cap ... perhaps their own tin helmet with two holes where a bullet had passed clear through without touching their head.

A clean handkerchief was almost symbolic, a touch of gentle English civilisation after barbarous experiences. There were much better things to come. The men were often filthy from the battlefield and their long, painful journey.

Once they had reached whichever of the Bristol hospitals they had been allocated, there was the relief of bathed wounds, a wash, a meal and a merciful change from soiled battledress into clean hospital uniform. Clean, everything clean. A clean mirror to shave in and clean, hot water. Clean sheets and pyjamas and clothes. Clean, beautifully clean skin rid of the lice of the trenches. Clean notepaper to write on. For the more severely injured, X-rays and immediate operations but still a quiet awakening into a sterilised, warm, comfortable world which helped many forget that there was a stump where there should have been a leg or a hollow which had held an eye only a few days before.

Once the euphoria of safety had died away, all wanted to see familiar faces and Bristol set up an organisation which registered the incoming wounded, contacted their relatives and arranged inexpensive lodgings for visiting families. The same groups interviewed the casualties about their front line experiences, finding where they'd fought, with which units and when. Each interview was checked against the official missing list to see if there was any useful information of the whereabouts or fate of lost soldiers.

A great deal of generosity was shown to families visiting their sick children or husbands, brothers or sweethearts. Helpers at one Bristol hospital were deeply moved when they found a mother in tears. She and her husband had arrived to sit by their critically injured 19-year-old son on Saturday to be told by the Medical Officer that the boy was unlikely to survive the weekend. By Monday morning, he was still alive but his father had to return to his job in another part of the country, or be thrown out of work. The mother was distraught. The case was immediately put before Bristol's voluntary care bureau and the mother stayed for nine weeks at the expense of local people. Her son lived.

If you made it to Bristol, you almost certainly survived your wounds, however severe. The figures are remarkable. The Beaufort War Hospital lost just 134 soldiers from 29,400 patients and Southmead's record was similar, with 192 losses from a total 37,397. Once you had recovered from the worst and reassured your friends and relatives that you were on the mend, then Bristol wasn't a bad place to be.

Some cities, particularly London, grew tired of playing host to the wounded and began to find them an embarrassing nuisance. Bristol never did. There were always entertainments and shows, free tickets to the theatres and cinemas, free entrance to the zoo in Clifton and an army of women and girls happy to cheer up morose youngsters. Bristol's magnificent singer Clara Butt gave frequent patriotic concerts in the city for the wounded men, her *Land of Hope and Glory* thrilling audiences into an ecstasy of emotion if only for an hour or two.

There were still larky moments for the boys. The word went around that London had set a record by clearing a theatre of 2,000 war wounded in an hour. Whatever London's injured could do, Bristol's could do better. So when the Bristol Hippodrome held two successive matinee performances of a show for the wounded, it was decided to have a crack at London's achievement. After the first afternoon performance, 2,270 men, 400 of them on crutches, were off the premises and on their way back to hospital within 52 minutes. As if that wasn't good enough, the next day's show, attended by 2,200 including 350 crutch cases, were out and away in just 37 minutes.

But larks and visits, shows and friendships and all the care in the world couldn't disguise the deeper tragedies. The nagging memories of lost pals and the thud-thud-thud of imagined guns would last for years, even for the least shell-shocked. Worst of all were the crippled and the horribly maimed, youths who had lost limbs and shuffled around like old men, tottering on crutches and false legs or confined to wheelchairs for the rest of their lives. However much the people of Bristol did for them in workshops and visits, expeditions and parties, they knew they faced a bleak future, whether the war ended or not.

They demanded dignity, respect and, if not a home fit for heroes, at least a job. And that was to prove a very difficult demand to answer.

SEVEN

November 1918: The Eleventh Hour

The Somme battles of 1916 did not bring the longed for breakthrough, despite appalling loss of life on all sides. The Third Battle of Ypres a year later was a British advance of a few kilometres that cost half a million casualties. The grisly stalemate seemed set to last forever.

But the situation began to change. On April 6th, 1917, the United States declared war on Germany. Even if the US army was small to start with, America's industry and rich economy provided much-needed weapons and cash. The Bolshevik Revolution of 1917 signalled the Russian collapse on the Eastern Front, freeing German troops for service in the West. Germany launched its final great offensive in early 1918, smashing a hole through the British lines on the Somme in an attempt to sever the French and British armies. At first the advance succeeded but then it began to run out of momentum. Tired, starving, demoralised German soldiers began looting shops and cellars, more interested in food and wine than in conquest. Britain, France and the United States counter-attacked, forcing the Germans into a retreat that eventually ground to a halt with stiffening resistance in October 1918. It looked like stalemate all over again.

But not for long. The German home front was in ruins, the people suffering great hardships and revolutionary factions, spurred on by the successes of their comrades in the new USSR, began to win greater support from hungry, disillusioned people.

Germany's allies fell by the wayside and the final straw was the mutiny of the German fleet. The Fatherland was on the brink of revolution and despite the continuing heroism and resistance of the army, the Generals reluctantly agreed to an Armistice.

Hostilities ceased at 11 a.m. on November 11th ... the

eleventh hour of the eleventh day of the eleventh month. The Allies were victorious. It was only later, years later, that everyone remembered the significance of two points: that the German army which surrendered was intact, and that most of its soldiers were still in positions on foreign soil.

'Bristol's Own' no longer existed at that historic moment. In August 1918 the 12th Gloucesters had helped capture part of the Arras–Albert railway line and before the end of the month, in the Allied advance, they had captured nine German officers and 300 other ranks of the enemy. The city's pals battalion last went into action in the final push forward by the Allies. On October 5th, 1918, 'Bristol's Own' received orders to disband and to transfer survivors to other units. On October 6th, after a Church parade, the unit ceased to exist.

The Great War, which had begun in such a fiercely patriotic spirit, had become loathsome. Bristolians hated the daily Roll of Honour in the local papers. Week after week they saw names of men they had known or whose families they knew. This wasn't glorious death. It was mass slaughter. Everyone was fed up with the restrictions imposed on their lives. They were tired of food shortages and poorly-lit streets.

Many were alarmed at the way society seemed to be drifting. They complained of a decline in moral standards and a rise in juvenile delinquency. Young teenagers in some parts of the city had become increasingly loutish and troublesome with their rowdy street gangs, rudeness to passers-by and alarming lack of discipline. It wasn't difficult to point to the war's disruption of family life and some even blamed the more sensational American films that were standard fare on Bristol's busy cinema circuit. As for the teenagers themselves ... they were terrified of the future.

Soldiers coming home to the West Country on leave were bitter at what they found. They saw women in the well-paid industrial jobs and businessmen and industrialists growing fat on the profits of war. They watched kids with money to burn misbehaving in public and, above all, they returned to an area that was clearly doing very nicely, thank you, despite inconveniences that seemed trivial to a man from the front.

The restrictions hadn't stopped the cinemas and theatres doing a roaring trade, the latter sometimes with fatuously patriotic music hall turns which held no appeal to troops in the audience. Soldiers left that sort of jingoistic claptrap to the civilians. *They* had enough to do keeping alive without worrying about such indulgences as idealism or love of country. The civilians didn't know the half of what was really happening in France and Flanders — and didn't want to know, local Tommies told each other. And it was all too often true. War-weariness had set in.

The Battle of the Somme's appalling cost in lives had shattered any lingering belief in the glamour of war. The Third Battle of Ypres in 1917 had added a nightmarish quality which people tried to shut out of their minds. What had happened that summer and autumn was the unimaginable.

'Bristol's Own', the 12th Gloucesters, had been pitched in at the height of the carnage around the remains of the tiny Belgian village of Passchendaele and fought there for 11 days. Four officers and 59 men were killed, six officers and 177 men wounded and four officers and 91 men gassed. Passchendaele. The very name spookily evoked spectres of Christ's Passion on Calvary.

When survivors did return to Bristol, wounded or on leave, they couldn't or wouldn't describe what they'd seen. They didn't tell mothers of their lost pals how they had drowned, cursing and shrieking, in stinking lakes of mud. It was better not to talk to fathers about the corpse-ridden, shell-pocked, gas-poisoned, waterlogged battlefield which had added a disgusting new dimension to the horrors of war. Soldiers with such experiences were men apart. They could only feel at ease with comrades who had shared such ordeals. The gulf between serviceman and civilian had become desperately wide and for many it would take years to bridge.

By 1918, Bristol's doubts and fears, bitterness and losses had worked themselves into an obsession . . . that the Great War was never going to end and that it was going to be a lasting part of the fabric of 20th century life. People began to believe that succeeding generations of young men would be doomed to be shipped out to the Continent like cattle to fight and die in huge battles in which armies would advance or retreat a few yards.

The chilling mood broke into terror when the Germans began their great offensive in the spring. For weeks it looked as if the Hun had broken through and the censored *Western Daily Press, Bristol Times and Mirror* and other local sheets had to work doubly hard to prevent utter demoralisation. The crisis passed and the sullen mood returned.

Food was in short supply and the city's shopping streets always had queues. The day a huge quantity of margarine was put on sale at the Corn Exchange someone counted 4,000 people in what was claimed to be the longest local queue of all. You rarely found bacon or butter. Meat was in short supply. Fish was very expensive and a scrawny little chicken cost half a guinea (52p), a lot of money then. People didn't like the rough war-time bread and many complained about the imported meat because it had been frozen. But if you were prepared to wait long enough, you could buy even rarer items. Hoarders spent hours queueing , triumphantly carrying off some prized foodstuff and then promptly joining the back of the next queue. Some Bristol women adopted a neat little ruse. They borrowed a friend's baby and began queueing with the howling infant in their arms. It usually did the trick, with sympathetic shoppers hurrying 'mother' to the head of the queue so she could return home quickly with her supposed child.

Something had to be done to prevent abuses. Free Trade may have been an act of faith in pre-war Britain, but it ran sharply against the war-time spirit of fair shares for all. Bristol intervened with its Food Committee. The Committee had originally been set up to fix prices and regulate supplies, thus stamping out the profiteering of the first days. In February 1918 the Committee was given powers to ration certain goods. The Government followed Bristol's model in the summer.

So State Control, which had already been introduced to speed up production and improve efficiency in the munitions industry, had been extended to the domestic consumer market. It was yet another of the war's changes which would have a lasting effect on British society.

The most noticeable change in Bristol in the summer of 1918 was not political though . . . it was the colourful arrival of increasing numbers of men from the United States. The Yanks kept coming and coming. On July 4th, 300 American soldiers and sailors stationed at Yate were invited to celebrate Independence Day in the city. They marched smartly through the main streets of Bristol to a noisy lunch at the Drill Hall in Old Market which had been decorated with the flags of the Allies. In August an even bigger contingent arrived. They had landed at Avonmouth docks and joined their troop train. It was halted at Clifton Down station and the men divided into two sections. They were marched down Whiteladies Road to the City Art Gallery where they were given a rousing welcome and generous refreshments before re-joining their train.

One or two of the optimists began to wonder if the omens for the future weren't starting to look rather good at last, and that feeling lasted through September and October. October turned to November and the news was suddenly, maddeningly, magnificently good. Germany's strength looked fragile. The Allies were advancing. The word on everyone's lips was . . . Armistice.

Such wonderful news from the Continent couldn't have been more needed. Bristolians were dying in their hundreds and this time not on the battlefields — but at home. A particularly virulent form of influenza had appeared among soldiers and sailors that spring. It spread across the country in the worst epidemic Britain had seen since the cholera plague of 1848. In the first week of October, four people died of the new 'flu in Bristol. In the week ending November 2nd, 197 died. The Chief Constable ordered cinemas to close between each show so that the auditoria could be thoroughly ventilated. Schools were shut to prevent infection spreading among children. Ventilation of all public buildings was ordered. The Tramways company was taken to task for allowing too many passengers on each vehicle, so increasing the risk of germs being passed on. There were some pitiful cases. One family of eight in east Bristol caught the 'flu. The father, mother and one of the children died. The five remaining orphans were left to the tender mercies of the Bristol Guardians of the poor.

The deaths at home echoed the deaths on the Western Front, because the killing had not abated. The daily Roll of Honour numbered hundreds and sometimes thousands as the Allies paid a high price for their advances. These last deaths at the front are some of the most poignant of the war. Within days people would bitterly think 'If only . . .'

Like the courageous Professor A.R. Skemp, Winterstoke Professor of English at Bristol University. It was announced on November 8th that he had been killed in action in France, leaving a widow and two children. Skemp had proved an invaluable help to the army as an instructor and his repeated requests to get back to the fighting were refused. At last, with an end to the war in sight, his superiors reluctantly relented and he was given permission to rejoin the Gloucestershire Regiment. It cost him his life.

On Saturday November 9th it was announced that the week's 'flu deaths were 187, a slight drop on the previous week's figure. It looked as if the worst might be over. That same day Frank Sheppard, Bristol's first-ever Labour Lord Mayor, ended his year in office. Sheppard had been a great success as the Chief Citizen and he had done as much as the many responsible trades union leaders to demonstrate that socialists were no longer on the fringe of politics. They were now part of the mainstream, and they were going to be badly needed to cope with the depression and unemployment that was about to come.

The day Frank Sheppard bowed out, the Government announced its plans for munitions workers during 'the abnormal period that must immediately follow on the cessation of hostilities'. Wages would be subsidised for the time being. 'If your earnings fall below 30s (£1.50) a week for men of 18, 15s (75p) for boys, 25s (£1.25) for women and 12s 6d (62p) for girls, the State will make up the rest'. The statement also announced that anyone thrown out of work by the munitions industry would receive 13 weeks' unemployment benefit.

Sunday November 10th, 1918 was a restless day. People were almost afraid to believe the best after what had seemed like an age of fear that the war would never end. There were echoes of that nervous tension that had marked the weekend the war began. And, just as they had done that August Bank Holiday weekend four years and three months before, people left the suburbs and began congregating on the City Centre to be near the newspaper offices.

The Monday morning papers carried a Roll of Honour as dreadful as any seen during the war. The Germans had been fighting back furiously and it was announced that 45 officers and 1,401 rank and file had been killed with 116 officers and 2,866 men wounded. It was impossible to concentrate on work. Crowds lingered around the Centre and the streets were full of children with nothing to do because of closed schools.

At 10.30 a.m. men hurried out of the newspaper offices with the stunning news. The Armistice was confirmed! Peace in half an hour's time! There was a moment of silence as the enormity of it all sank in. It was the last silence heard in Bristol for days.

The pent-up emotions of more than four years of war erupted as the news spread like wildfire across the city. Flags and bunting suddenly appeared as if from nowhere. Factories and offices emptied magically. The streets became great seas of people, the crowds so dense that public transport ground to a halt. The noise of the crowds could be heard by the Bristol Appeals Tribunal as it sat down to another day's work. There were two long lists of men who had appealed against call-up. Ald. John Swaish turned to his fellow Tribunal members with a smile. 'I think we shall make ourselves look ridiculous in the eyes of the public if we order any men into the Army' he said. Swaish suspended the Tribunal *sine die* ... and within hours the Government announced that there would be no further conscription. Ald. H.W. Twiggs, Bristol's new Lord Mayor, had planned to announce a public holiday when the news came through but Bristol had decided to take one anyway.

The first to give some sort of semblance of order to the raucous, impromptu dancing and shouting were the lads of the Bristol University-based Officers Training Corps. They formed themselves into a parade and began marching down Park Street followed by crowds of graduates and under-graduates from the university, most of them girls. The boys of nearby Bristol Grammar School quickly joined in the fun, hastily assembling the school band and then marching down after the OTC and university party to the centre. They carried a scarecrow effigy of the Kaiser which was later burnt to whoops and howls of delight.

Everyone fell about laughing at the touching sight of about 50 street urchins, barefoot, grimy and badly clothed who began marching up Park Street. The two boys in front had managed to filch some of the bunting which was hurriedly being hung from office windows and strung across streets, and they carried it head high. Behind them came four boys who'd rigged up some old biscuit tins as impromptu drums and were banging them noisily.

Any vehicle which did manage to make any sort of process through the crowds was immediately commandeered as piles of fun-seekers scrambled on for a free ride. Army and Navy lorries slowly drove along loaded with wounded Tommies, girls and children all waving their arms off.

The more spirited soldiers jumped onto the running boards of vans and cars. In Wine Street, one tommy made a leap for a running board, overbalanced and fell into the lap of two astonished officers. Once they'd recovered from their surprise they joined in the fun, pretending to cradle the lad like a baby. The crowds loved that. Four American servicemen paraded in Clare Street and Corn Street, bearing a huge Stars and Stripes and loudly singing *Rule Britannia* while waving Union Jacks in their spare hands. Everyone looked up as an aeroplane swooped so low over the City Centre that you could see the face of the pilot and his companion, grinning down on the wild scenes below them.

Freedom ruled. Church bells rang as evening fell and the sky was lit up by bonfires, which had been banned for years. Fog sirens were sounded, hooters hooted and more and more lights came on. Everywhere were dancing masses of soldiers and sailors with girls on their arms and groups of women and girls ranging the streets determinedly kissing and embracing every wounded soldier they could find.

Bristol's industrial and financial leaders ended the war where they had begun it, in the Commercial Rooms in Corn Street. The Bishop, the Lord Mayor and the Sheriff were there, too. The Bishop led the singing of the Doxology ... 'Praise God from whom all blessings flow', they all sang. Some wept quietly at the pity of it all and thought of the boys who would never come home. The tears might have run down their cheeks a little faster if they had known how much the home-coming troops would hate and despise them and their generation for sending them to war while they stayed at home to make handsome profits.

The celebrations didn't end that night of Monday November 11th. They went on in Bristol for days. The noisiest, wildest day of all was Tuesday November 12th. The tens of thousands who had been marooned in the suburbs when the public transport system had ground to a halt the day before were determined to celebrate too. There were even greater crowds, exulting in freedom after what they now called 'the war to end all wars'. It was marvellous to be able to flout D.O.R.A. People climbed lamp-posts and rubbed away the blue paint from the street lights. The bell ringers were out in force again. And in the unaccustomed crescendo of noise and light that night, all you could see were great crowds dancing and running, walking and singing against a backdrop of blazing light and waving flags and bunting.

The First World War was over.

EPILOGUE

On February 15, 1919, Bristol paid tribute to some of its best-known war heroes.

Five of the city's six Victoria Cross winners together with a further 250 officers and men who had won decorations were invited to an assembly at the Colston Hall. The soldiers and ex-servicemen gathered at the Drill Hall in Old Market and then marched behind the band of the Gloucestershire Regiment to the ceremony. The streets were lined with waving, cheering people. The Colston Hall was decked with flags of the Allies and, after everyone had sung the National Anthem, the Lord Mayor, Ald. H.W. Twiggs, stepped forward to read aloud a message that had just arrived from Buckingham Palace. It was a personal letter from the King.

'I desire you to congratulate all those whom you are honouring today on their magnificent achievement and, at the same time, I wish to associate myself with the feelings of pride aroused in the hearts of our fellow citizens at the splendid record of Bristol's gallant sons, who have added fresh lustre to your city's great traditions'.

Each of the VC winners was given a gold watch and an illuminated address and the ceremony was rounded off with yet another rousing performance of the National Anthem.

Afterwards, as people walked away, there was talk about the various plans for a war memorial to honour the dead just as they had honoured the living.

The 'flu epidemic had petered out, its final toll about 1,000. A general election had returned Lloyd George. Men had begun coming home, but it was not to that much-vaunted home fit for heroes. Post-war Bristol was a depression-hit city, its thriving war-time industries wrecked by peace.

Of the returning soldiers, the lucky ones were those who had left steady jobs to fight for King and Country. Many employers had promised to keep places open for them, and most stuck by their word. The unlucky ones were those who had been drafted into the army without any training in commerce or industry. It was hard enough to find work for those returning to jobs, let alone this new, ill-educated, brutalised generation whose only practical lessons in life had been on the battlefield.

Ironies multiplied. The women, who'd been so loudly praised for all their help during the war, were thrown out of work as quickly as possible. Some were allowed to stay in clerical jobs because they had become so poorly paid that men no longer wanted to usurp them. Others dug their heels in and refused to quit, causing returning Tommies to complain bitterly about 'flappers' who had stolen their jobs while they fought in the trenches.

The understanding between labour and management disappeared. As unemployment grew and the fat war-time contracts ran out, the owners no longer needed the help of the workers' representatives. Why negotiate when there were precious few jobs and hosts of homecoming men to fill them? Fair shares for all, protection for the weak, a new sense of equality, the common purpose, the new woman. Had the war's changes all been just a great illusion to be swept aside as the old order and the old certainties took the reins once more? It certainly looked like it for a while, but the mood did not last. Society had changed drastically, despite all the efforts to reimpose the lost values of Edwardian society.

You can see it in our lives today. The legacy lingers, its most potent and obvious reminders in those pathetic war memorials to long-forgotten men you will find in civic parks and village churchyards, town squares and city centres, all bearing stirring lines like 'Lest We Forget'. There is British Summer Time. Our pub licensing hours. Even the popularity of cigarette smoking. All date from the First World War.

It does not take long to recognise the deeper changes. They are in our outlook and attitudes and the society we live in, and the social revolution which brought those changes was hurried along by the war. A dislike of servility. A distrust of the Press. The emancipation of women. Suspicion of those who give orders. A far less rigid class structure. Powerful trades unions. A confident working class. Permissiveness in sexual morality. A strong Labour party. The list goes on and on.

The years 1914–1918 mark a watershed that separates the sunset of Victorian/Edwardian Britain from the dawn of the 20th century. At its most extreme, compare the prim, chaperoned, middle-class Miss of 1913 with the Flapper of 1923. The two might have come from different planets.

If I had to choose a single event that marks the bitter moment when the door slammed in the face of Edwardian Britain, I would pick the Battle of the Somme, that months-long series of brutal engagements which began 70 years ago on July 1st, 1916. It remains one of the great horror stories of British history. It was when Britain's huge volunteer army, young, hopeful, patriotic and keen were led at walking pace, weighed down with packs of equipment, straight into the jaws of industrialised slaughter of undreamt-of efficiency. Something like 65,000 of them were killed or injured in the first day and their innocence died with them.

Lt.-Col. Martin Archer Shee, the man who had commanded the Bristol's 'pals' battalion, returned to the Somme in the early 1920s to erect a tall wooden cross at Longueval, the place where the 12th Gloucesters had begun their dreadful spell of service at the battlefront in the early days of the great slaughter. In 1930, some of the survivors of 'Bristol's Own' made a pilgrimage to France to remember their fallen friends and to place flowers around the memorial. The original cross has since vanished, its fate as unknown as that of the missing whose deaths it commemorated as well as the deaths and injuries to scores more Bristol men who fought near the spot. At the time of writing, plans are almost complete to re-erect a facsimile on the cross-roads where 'Bristol's Own' began their first large-scale action.

On June 26th, 1932, Bristol at last unveiled its main war memorial on the City Centre. It is an impressive piece of architecture, simple, dignified and somehow creating an atmosphere of silence and stillness even at the busiest times. The terrible irony of the ceremony and the war it recalled was that the killing was not over. It was barely half run.

Ten days before Sir William Birdwood pulled back the flags to reveal the monument, the German government had lifted its ban on the Nazi party's stormtroopers. By the day of the Bristol ceremony, Germany was embroiled in a bloody election campaign. The servicemen and veterans, widows and onlookers who were there to see Bristol's 4,000 war dead honoured were thinking of German dead too ... not the Germans who had died in the trenches 14 and more years before but the 80 or so who had been killed and the hundreds who had been injured already that month in the violent political street battles that were raging across the Fatherland. The spectre of German militarism was beginning to haunt Europe once again as Adolf Hitler, who had faced battalions like 'Bristol's Own' at Ypres, continued a march to power that would win him the Chancellorship of Germany by the New Year. As Hitler said, the German army had not been defeated, not been routed, not been destroyed. History would make amends for that before long.

When war did come to Bristol again, there was no mafficking, there were no triumphant crowds, there was no flag-waving and there were no young men marching up and down the streets singing patriotic songs. Instead a bitter, heart-breaking sense of despair that the whole bloody business was starting all over again ... and that this time the realities of war would come home to the city itself. On the very first day of the Second World War, an air raid siren sounded in Bristol.

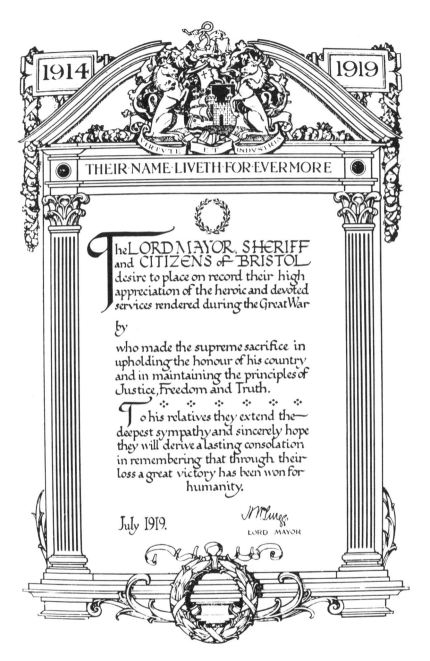

THEIR·NAME·LIVETH·FOR·EVERMORE

The LORD MAYOR, SHERIFF and CITIZENS of BRISTOL desire to place on record their high appreciation of the heroic and devoted services rendered during the Great War

by

who made the supreme sacrifice in upholding the honour of his country and in maintaining the principles of Justice, Freedom and Truth.

To his relatives they extend the deepest sympathy and sincerely hope they will derive a lasting consolation in remembering that through their loss a great victory has been won for humanity.

July 1919.

H.W. Twiggs
LORD MAYOR

The certificate presented by Bristol's Lord Mayor Ald. H.W. Twiggs to relatives of the 4,000 Bristolians killed during the Great War.

BRISTOL BOOKS

Redcliffe are the leading publishers of books about Bristol, having produced nearly fifty on different aspects of the city's life and history, over the last ten years. No other British city outside London has received such attention. This is both a measure of the richness and significance of Bristol's past and present, and of the intense pride and interest of Bristolians in their own city.

Redcliffe combines the very best in writing, research and illustration with high quality design and printing. The result is a wide and surprising range of books from 50p to £10.00, which are always tremendous value for money.

We are always willing to consider fresh ideas for new books. If you would like a copy of our complete list, which includes books about Bath, the West Country and Art and Literature, please send a SAE to:

Redcliffe Press Ltd
49 Park Street
Bristol
BS1 5NT

The following are a few examples of our books:

BRISTOL BETWEEN THE WARS Ed. David Harrison   *£3.50*

Bristol has never seen such years of change as those between the two World Wars, changes mirrored in this compelling account.

This frank, intimate book, richly illustrated with rare, archive photographs, captures a permanent record of a period rapidly slipping beyond personal experience.

BRISTOL: MARITIME CITY by Frank Shipsides and Robert Wall   *£10.00*

The epic story of the Port of Bristol is recalled from the earliest times, when man first set out to tame the formidable Severn estuary through the turbulent centuries of English history right up to the current 20th century controversies over the new Royal Portbury Dock.

The book is essential reading for all lovers of Bristol, and for those who admire and seek to understand her greatness.

JOHN CABOT by Bryan Little £1.50

Authentic material about John Cabot, one of the great figures in Britain's maritime history, is very scarce. Drawing on largely inaccessible and out-of-print material, historian Bryan Little has brought together the genuine facts about Cabot's life and achievements in Italy, the Near East, Bristol and North America.

THE BRISTOL SCENE by Jennifer Gill £1.25

A fascinating glimpse of how the city looked in the early nineteenth century, just before the advent of the camera.

Many of the illustrations are from the priceless Braikenridge Collection in the City Art Gallery. George Weare Braikenridge, a retired merchant and plantation owner, had antiquarian interests, and commissioned nearly 1,500 drawings by local artists of Bristol between 1818 and 1830.

THE BRISTOL HOUSE by Keith Mallory £6.50

A lavish survey of the development of the riches of Bristol's domestic architecture. From medieval buildings, Georgian terraces, Victorian villas and artisan terraces, through to the twentieth century and contemporary design. Over 130 illustrations.

BRISTOL BLITZ DIARY by John Dike £2.95

The chance discovery of a faded old memorandum book has provided a fascinating insight into the German air raids on the city of Bristol.

The diary provides us with a minute-by-minute, bomb-by-bomb, street-by-street account, illustrated with many photographs, several of which are previously unpublished.

GONE FOR GOOD Tales from a Bristol Boyhood
by Lewis Wilshire   *£2.50*

Fifteen delightful 'yarns' about characters and places long
since vanished, seen through the innocent, enquiring eyes of
the 'young' Lewis Wilshire, who is the popular story-teller on
BBC Radio Bristol.

"Never again", says the author, "will there be such
characters. They were originals, living our their comic,
tragic, earthy lives in a lamp-lit, shadowy world."

BRISTOL OBSERVED by J H Bettey   *£3.95*

The evolving city as seen through the eyes of visitors to
Bristol from medieval times to the present day. Accounts by,
among others, Samuel Pepys, Elizabeth I, J.B. Priestley,
Robert Southey and Daniel Defoe, and previously unpublished historical documents, reveal exactly what they saw as
outsiders, which enables us to see the city today in a new
light. Fully illustrated with antique maps and prints.

A CITY AND ITS CINEMAS by Charles Anderson   *£2.95*

The Rise and Fall of Bristol's picture houses. The author
draws on the personal reminiscences of local people who, as
patrons and staff, remember the heady days when the
shuffling queues were an essential part of a Saturday
evening out.

An important section on William Friese-Green casts
doubt on the contribution which the Bristol-born inventor is
popularly believed to have made to the development of
cinematography.

PORTRAIT OF A ZOO by Robert and Anne Warin
Foreword by Gerald Durrell   *£2.95*

Published to mark the 150th birthday of this world famous
zoo. The authors trace the history and development of the
zoo which closely reflect changes in attitudes to wildlife and
conservation in the world as a whole.

Liberally spiced with hilarious and fascinating 'inside'
stories, and many remarkable photographs.